P9-CFG-274

# COOKING
## from THE HIP

Fast Easy Phenomenal Meals

# COOKING
## from THE HIP

## Cat Cora

with Ann Krueger Spivack

PHOTOGRAPHS BY DEBORAH JONES

HOUGHTON MIFFLIN COMPANY   BOSTON   NEW YORK   2007

Visit our Web site: www.houghtonmifflinbooks.com.

Library of Congress Cataloging-in-Publication Data

Cora, Cat.
    Cooking from the hip : fast, easy, phenomenal meals / Cat Cora
with Ann Krueger Spivack.
        p.  cm.
    Includes bibliographical references and index.
    ISBN-13: 978-0-618-72990-6
    ISBN-10: 0-618-72990-9
    1. Cookery, American.    2. Cookery, International.
3. Quick and easy cookery.    4. Cookery (Leftovers)
I. Spivack, Ann Krueger.    II. Title.
    TX715.C7945 2007
    641.5'973—dc22        2006026929

Book design by Anne Chalmers
Food styling by Amy Nathan
Prop styling by Carol Hacker

Printed in China
C&C 10 9 8 7 6 5 4 3 2 1

This book is dedicated to
my mother and father,
who showed me that there is
no end to a woman's growth,

and to Jennifer and Zoran,
who grow with me every day.

## A SPECIAL THANK-YOU

Just as we started this book, Hurricane Katrina hit my home state of Mississippi. Because of my charity organization, Chefs for Humanity, and my television work on *Iron Chef America*, I was privileged to go into some of the most devastated areas—privileged because I got a chance to pitch in and help. I felt lucky to cook for some of those amazing, heroic rescue workers. At one point, I was cooking opposite Chef Ming Tsai in the Bayou View Elementary School's kitchen in Gulfport. Both of us were working feverishly, using cafeteria pots and pans and any food that came in as donations from large food companies, individuals, and the restaurants and casinos in the area. Suddenly cooking wasn't a way of earning a living or even something I do because I love it. Cooking was a way to help. That was the high point of my career.

When you come back home from that—and you have a home to return to—you take a fresh look at your kitchen. You look at your full cupboards and shining pots, and you have a sense that you can cook anytime under any circumstances. I am inspired by the many people who are aiding the recovery of the regions hit by Katrina. My thanks to these people are deep and heartfelt.

Cat Cora
Chefs for Humanity
www.chefsforhumanity.org

# Acknowledgments

This book would never have been written without the support of my family. To Jen, my one true love and constant source of strength and patience, none of this would have been possible without you. All my accomplishments are our accomplishments. To Zoran, my little Greek god, who makes me laugh every day and reminds me that being a mom is my most important purpose in life.

To Mom and Dad, who nurture me through the hard times and celebrate with me through the good times. You are always there, and I thank you. To my grandmom, Alma, I know you are still with me every day, helping me along my journey. To my brothers, Mike and Chris, I don't get to see you as often as I want, but you are always in my heart. To Carrie and Jennifer, thank you again for bringing my brothers joy and for bringing Nicholas, Alexis, Anna, Andrew, Paxton, and Morgan into the world.

To my godparents, Taki and Maria, for all your teachings and love through the years. To Carla and Randy, for being the best in-laws a girl could have. To my great brother-in-law, Jeff, and to Joanne, Terry, Jason, Kim, Judy, Scott, Jan, and Web, my extended family and southern soul patrol. To my aunt, Demetra, my uncle, George (rest his soul), and cousins Yanni and Eleni in Skopelos, Greece, for treasuring my family as we do you. Finally, to all my friends in Mississippi, I am always here for you and miss you like crazy.

Thank you to Sasha Bernstein, my trusted assistant, who makes my professional world a brighter place and keeps me sane.

I owe many, many thanks to the people who helped create this book: Ann Krueger Spivack, a writer who knows me so well and captures my voice like no one else can. Thank you for being my director and the driving force on this book.

To my agent, Doe Coover, who pushed my concept and accepted only the best in a publisher. To Rux Martin, for whom I have the utmost respect and admiration, thank you for embracing *Cooking from the Hip*. To my trusted friend Terry Paetzold, who has tested both of my books, thanks especially for the Potato–Celery Root Soup and the Endive, Honeydew, and Pear Salad.

Deborah Jones, I knew I just had to have you photograph my book. Your work is so organic and visceral. You truly know how to capture a chef's spirit. Thanks also to super-stylist Amy Nathan, who made my recipes look gorgeous, to Carol Hacker for the just-right props, and to Jeri Jones, who kept us all going during the photo shoots.

To everyone at Houghton Mifflin, especially Mimi Assad, for carrying the Lemonade Cookies when she rode her bike to work; Anne Chalmers, for the beautiful interior design; and Michaela Sullivan, for the cover. Also, thanks to Deborah DeLosa, Houghton Mifflin's director of cookbook publicity; to Susan Dickinson for her fine, thoughtful copyedit; to Jessica Sherman and Janet McDonald for their careful proofreading; and to Liz Duvall for guiding the pages through the process with warmth and humor.

Thanks to Jaime Wolf, my legal rock and friend, who keeps me in good graces and out of hot water. Jason Hodes, my agent, or, better yet, my professional Buddha, thank you for all your hard work, honesty, and dedication.

David Greenblatt, my manager, I thank you for all your guidance and direction and for being such a fun foodie to eat with. Jon Rosen, thank you for seeing into the future and believing in my vision. Thanks to David Palmer for being not only one of the most stylish agents around but also a great friend.

Jeff Googel and Betsy Berg, thanks for all that you do for me day to day. Staci Wolfe, Jackie Crystal, Greg Longstreet, and the Polaris PR team, thanks for always helping me look my best and getting me into great Hollywood parties. Thanks to the folks at Triage for their support and friendship.

Thanks to Barbara Fairchild, Amy Foster, and the *Bon Appétit* family for appointing me executive chef and making me feel welcome.

Debra Rainey, executive director of Chefs for Humanity, thanks for your unconditional professionalism, dedication, and passion for the organization. You are truly an amazing soul. Thanks to the Chefs for Humanity culinary council: Ming Tsai, Charlie Ayers, Gale Gand, Rick Bayless, Joanne Boundy, Art Smith, Robert St. John, Elizabeth Falkner, Bobby Flay, Grant MacPherson, Marcus Samuelsson, Tim

Scott, and Norman Van Aken. Thanks to the Chefs for Humanity team: Janet Fouts, Dina Ross, Marvin Nyman, Maryann Baietti, Jim Swenson, Christi Malvezzi, and Dr. Virginia Lee Cora.

Thanks to David Dodson: I'm glad we always look out for each other. To my trusted friend LoriLynn Bauer: I'm sure we will be cane-racing one day as we grow into old friends. Catrina Lembo Di Martini, Randy Di Martini, and Nicki D, you are friends for life. Laura Buckley, thanks for always being a good friend and letting me be a friend to you.

With much gratitude to Georges Blanc, one of the two chefs who allowed me to apprentice with him in Vonnas in the Bresse region of France. Working with this master of cuisine changed how I look at food. Chef Roger Vergé had a hug for me every day when I apprenticed at Moulin de Mougins. He, his wife, Denise, and his chef, Serge, left an imprint on my life through their farms, their food, and their wine. His love of the good life has stayed with me. Much gratitude to Julia Child, who kindly took the time to talk to me many years ago. Her advice to attend the Culinary Institute of America was the first step of my career. To me, she will always be the First Lady, and her love of food inspired and paved the way for so many other cooks.

Thank you to Jacques Pépin for sending a letter on my behalf to the Beard House after tasting a meal that I cooked at Don Giovanni's. Jacques has been a constant source of inspiration since I began cooking.

Thanks to all my friends at the Food Network: Bruce Seidel, Jill Novatt, Carrie Welch, Lauren Mueller, Brook Johnson, Bob Tuschman, Alison Page, Susan Stockton, and all the great culinary and production crews I have had the good fortune to work with. To all the boys at Reveille Productions, I can't wait for the next project.

Many thanks to Nick Boer and the *Contra Costa Times*. Nick inspired me by making my newspaper column, "Cooking from the Hip," such a blast to write.

And, last but not least, to my *Iron Chef America* teammates, Bobby Flay, Mario Batali, and Morimoto, thanks for giving me a heads-up that it would be the fastest hour of my life!

Introduction xii

Resources for Ingredients 245
Index 246

Fast 1

Easy 50

Fun 102

Phenomenal 174

Good to Know 228

# Introduction

Every time you open the refrigerator and your cupboards and put together a meal—even something as simple as bread and cheese and a salad—you are cooking from the hip. With this book, I'm hoping to expand your options, share a few of my tricks, and take you to a place where you feel comfortable winging it, even when guests are coming for dinner.

Cooking on *Iron Chef America* honed my own ability to cook from the hip. Improvising in the kitchen is partly a question of skills, but it's largely a matter of attitude. You can make the mental shift so that preparing a good home-cooked meal every night isn't a chore but a time to be with your family. Learn how to let them help you, all the while making it fun. There are never enough chances in this fast-paced world to connect with friends and family, and cooking gives you an opportunity to do just that. If I pass along only one thought—let your family and friends help you make dinner—this book will be a success for me.

While traveling across the country, I get to talk with lots of home cooks. And in every town, from Jackson to Las Vegas, Ann Arbor to Austin, the same questions come up again and again: Do you cook differently when you're eating with your son? What do you do with leftovers? What's the easiest thing you make at home? What do you make when friends come for dinner?

This book answers those questions while sharing my "go with what you've got" philosophy. Cooking from the hip means being flexible. It means using what's on hand and not being afraid to substitute ingredients. Cooking is like exercising. If you come at it with the idea that it can be fun and creative, then suddenly it becomes the high point in your day instead of a chore.

If you have a couple cans of beans in your pantry, some fresh mint, and a bottle of sherry vinegar, you can make a refreshing (and refreshingly easy) salad. Have a day-old baguette and some summer tomatoes? Make bruschetta. I'll show you how to cook from the hip using leftover rice from Chinese takeout and how to jazz up a fast stir-fry by adding fresh peaches or mangoes. I'll also show you how to get your hands dirty by slathering a quick herbal paste on a pork roast for a spectacular Porchetta that your guests will long remember. And when life gives you lemonade concentrate, make Lemonade Cookies—they'll take you only about fifteen minutes! I'll share what I keep in my own pantry at home and show you how to put together a meal that's fast, easy, fun to make, or phenomenal, for those occasions when you want to pull out all the stops.

A woman in a bookstore in Oxford, Mississippi, told me, "I want to put a meal on the table that doesn't embarrass me in front of my friends, but I don't want to spend my whole Saturday in the kitchen." *Cooking from the Hip* is for her—and for all the other home cooks who requested meals that are both simple and sensational. This book aims to cut down steps, combine just a few ingredients in creative, inventive ways, and, most important, change your mind-set about cooking being a solitary activity. Some of my favorite family meals call for my family to help prepare them. Take a sushi party, for example.

"Uh-oh," you're thinking. "Raw fish. I don't want to deal with that." OK, so skip the raw fish. Fill your rice rolls with mango chunks and teriyaki chicken. Or fill them with feta cheese, chopped cucumber, roasted red pepper, and kalamata olives. (I call that one the Zoran Roll, because my son fell in love with this when he was only eighteen months old.) Your sushi can be anything you want it to be. The trick to sushi is good rice, which I'll show you how to make. You put out the rice, fill small bowls with ingredients that you know your family will love (getting in as many veggies as possible), then roll, baby, roll. Everybody makes their own meal, and it's fun, easy on your budget, and nutritious. We have at least one "sushi (without the fish) bar" every month at my house. I'll give you lots of suggestions for what you can put in your sushi. Try it, and you'll find it becomes a staple at your house too.

My favorite recipes—the ones I make for my own family—have to be fast and easy. My Watermelon Gazpacho has brilliant color and terrific flavor—and it's a blast to whip up watermelon in a blender. You'll find out how to make Smoked Salmon Rillettes and Dilled Yogurt, a savory spread that's great the day after salmon and bagels. You're using your leftovers, making a dish that impresses your friends, and, best of all, spending less than five minutes in the kitchen, because your food processor does all the work.

That's the heart of this book. These recipes are simple to make and offer lots of ideas for pulling in leftovers. They'll wow your friends and even get your kids to eat better foods. The book is divided into four sections: Fast, Easy, Fun, and Phenomenal. You can turn to the section that suits your mood, whether you need dinner on the table in twenty minutes or fantastic recipes for a spur-of-the-moment Friday night get-together.

Most of us, especially in households with kids, tend to fall back on the same recipes over and over. I've written this book to give you more than new recipes—I want to change your attitude about dinnertime. I want to offer ideas that let you come home from a hard day at work and look forward to making dinner, instead of ordering a pizza. I want to encourage you to set up adult time—and some special adult foods—so that when you go back to parenting, you're rejuvenated. Time is what we Americans most lack—and yet the families who cook together and spend time together at the table are healthier and happier. Can a cookbook make you and your family healthier and happier? Let's just say that encouraging you to spend time together in the kitchen and around the table is a great place to start.

Cat Cora

Start with the very best ingredients—

fresh, beautiful vegetables, terrific ahi tuna,

chicken, pork, or lamb—and dinner can be

on the table in about 30 minutes, or even less.

Fast

## Appetizers

Crisped Bagel Chips   3

Smoked Salmon Rillettes
   and Dilled Yogurt   4

Medjool Dates with Goat Cheese
   and Toasted Almonds   7

Sweet Potato and Scallion Latkes   8

## Salads and Soups

Strawberry Arugula Salad   10

Orange, Fennel, and Olive Salad   12

Tomato and Shellfish Soup   15

## Main Dishes

Parmesan, Prosciutto, and Arugula Sandwich   16

Greek Lamb and Olive Burgers with Garlic "Sauce"   18

Over-the-Top Ahi Tuna Salad   21

Spicy Chicken and Peach (or Mango) Stir-Fry   23

Pork Skewers with Avocado Tzatziki   27

Creamy Fettuccine with Sausage, Olives, and Broccoli
   Rabe   29

Mussels with Saffron Wine Broth and Penne   33

COOKING WITHOUT MEASURING: Saffron Honey-
   Roasted Chicken   35

Lamb Chops with Asparagus-Feta Salsa Verde   37

Pan-Seared Filet of Beef with Corn Basil Succotash   39

## Side Dishes

Curried Broccoli Salad   40

Three-Bean Salad with Fresh Mint   43

Two-Bean Salad with Hearts of Palm and
   Blue Cheese   44

Orzo with Asiago Cheese   45

## Desserts

Chocolate Brownie Cupcakes
   with Seven-Minute Frosting   46

Mildred's Date Bars   49

# Fast

# Crisped Bagel Chips ·

I keep mini bagels in my freezer just for making these chips. Bagels can be stored for a long time in the freezer, so you can stock up at the bagel shop. Just be sure to slice them *before* freezing. Never attempt to slice a whole frozen bagel, because it's a surefire way to cut yourself. Use a serrated knife to cut the bagels slowly and carefully before freezing, or better yet, invest in a bagel cutter, which keeps your fingers safe and sound.

These crisp, garlicky chips are perfect with Smoked Salmon Rillettes (page 4), dips, and cheese, but they also put a whole new spin on chicken salad or tuna salad.

10 1-ounce frozen mini bagels, thawed
¼ cup extra-virgin olive oil
 2 garlic cloves, minced

Preheat the oven to 350°F.

Slice each bagel crosswise into 4 thin rounds. Toss the bagel slices, olive oil, and garlic together in a large bowl.

Arrange the bagel slices on a baking sheet, cut sides up, in a single layer. Bake for 12 minutes, or until the slices are crisp. Let cool. Slide the crisps onto a platter or into a bowl and serve. If you have leftover crisps, wrap them in plastic or keep in an airtight container. Reheat for 2 to 3 minutes in a 350°F oven before serving.

# Smoked Salmon Rillettes and Dilled Yogurt

I often set out an easy Sunday spread of smoked salmon, bagels, cream cheese, capers, tomatoes, and thinly sliced red onions. I came up with salmon rillettes as a way to use up the leftovers. Traditionally rillettes is a paste made from meat or fish. My version is like a tartare: easy, light, and delicious with bagel chips. You also can serve it with mixed greens as a dinner salad. It's worth making the aïoli for this recipe, but if you have cream cheese or crème fraîche on hand, by all means use what you have.

1/2 pound smoked salmon

1/2 small red onion, finely chopped

1 tablespoon finely chopped chives or scallions (green tops only)

1/4 cup drained and coarsely chopped capers

2 tablespoons Easy Aïoli (page 238), light mayonnaise, cream cheese, or crème fraîche, homemade (page 239) or store-bought

1 tablespoon fresh lemon juice
  Kosher salt and freshly ground black pepper
  Dill fronds for garnish (optional)
  Crisped Bagel Chips (page 3), pita chips, crackers, or baguette slices
  Dilled Yogurt (page 6)

Cat's Note  I like to chop the onion, chives, and capers by hand and then mix them with the salmon, which I've minced in the food processor. Ann likes to chop the onion coarsely first, then toss everything in the food processor and whip it around. While her way is much faster and easier, you don't have the nice flecks of color from the chopped veggies, but she points out that her guests are too busy scarfing it down to miss the subtle colors.

Mince the salmon by hand or in a food processor. In a medium bowl, mix the salmon, onion, chives, capers, aïoli, and lemon juice. Season with salt and pepper to taste. Refrigerate until ready to serve.

Mound the rillettes on a serving platter. Garnish with dill fronds, if using. Serve with bagel chips, pita chips, crackers, or baguette slices. Have your guests top their rillettes with a spoonful of dilled yogurt.

## Dilled Yogurt

For the dilled yogurt, I prefer to strain the yogurt through a cheesecloth for 30 minutes. (If you don't have cheesecloth, just spoon the yogurt into a fine-mesh strainer set over a bowl or cup.) Strained yogurt means a thicker, creamier sauce, but you can skip the straining if you don't have time. Any extra yogurt can be refrigerated and used the next day in chicken salad.

¹/₄ cup plain low-fat yogurt, strained (see above)

2 tablespoons finely chopped fresh dill

3–4 tablespoons fresh lemon juice

Kosher salt and freshly ground black pepper

In a small bowl, mix the yogurt, chopped dill, lemon juice, and salt and pepper to taste.

# Medjool Dates with Goat Cheese and Toasted Almonds

I've been serving these dates for many years, and they're still a staple when I need a quick sweet with a cheese course or a snack for my son, Zoran. I served them at my first James Beard dinner, and they were a huge hit. Medjool dates are among the largest and most succulent dates. You'll find them in the produce section in the grocery store, often near the nuts.

Arrange them on a small plate for two people and serve with a glass of wine or make them the center of a cheese course. I love them with Classic Mojitos (page 116).

Dates can keep for quite a while, so they're a good pantry item. Look for plump dates with smooth, glossy skin. Avoid those that are broken, dry, shriveled, or sugary-looking. Sealed in an airtight plastic container or a resealable plastic bag, dates will last in your refrigerator for up to 6 months.

6 Medjool dates

6 whole almonds, toasted (see note)

6 tablespoons soft fresh goat cheese (about two 2-ounce rounds)

Make a slit in each date lengthwise and remove the seed. Slide in an almond and use a small spoon to fill the date with cheese. Gently squeeze the date closed with your fingers.

## Cat's Note

You can toast nuts easily on a baking sheet in a 400°F oven or in a small pan on the stove over medium heat. Stay close, since it's easy to overcook them. Use your sense of smell rather than your eyes to decide when they're done. As soon as you begin to smell the nuts' fragrance, remove them from the oven or the pan.

OPTION 1: With Lemon

If you can get Meyer lemons, substitute a long, thin strip of the peel (with the white pith scraped away) for the goat cheese. This combination is light and fragrant.

OPTION 2: With Prosciutto and Gorgonzola

Stuff the dates with a 1-inch strip of prosciutto and a tablespoon of Gorgonzola cheese.

# Sweet Potato and Scallion Latkes

Crispy outside, tender inside, these latkes are so good, I've had people follow me into the kitchen and beg me to make another batch so they can see how I do it. Based on traditional potato pancakes, these are easy and versatile too. You can serve them plain or sprinkled with chives or topped with a little crème fraîche and some smoked trout.

If you use about a tablespoon of the sweet potato, egg, and flour mixture, the latkes will be just the right size to pick up from a cocktail tray and eat with your fingers. If you want them larger, plate them and eat with a knife and fork.

1 pound sweet potatoes, peeled (about 2 medium)

2 large eggs, lightly beaten

½ cup plus 2 teaspoons all-purpose flour

1 teaspoon kosher salt

½ teaspoon freshly ground black pepper

2 scallions, finely chopped

About ½ cup vegetable oil for frying

3 tablespoons chopped fresh chives or scallions for garnish, or ½ cup crème fraîche, homemade (page 239) or store-bought, and ¼ pound smoked trout (available in large supermarkets)

Grate the sweet potatoes, using the large holes on a box grater or the grater disk of a food processor, and set aside.

In a large bowl, whisk together the eggs, flour, salt, and pepper. Add the sweet potatoes and the scallions and mix until the potatoes are well coated.

Heat 3 to 4 tablespoons of the oil in a 12-inch nonstick skillet over medium-high heat until the oil is hot but not smoking. Spoon 1 tablespoon of the potato mixture into the oil and flatten with a spatula to about 3 inches in diameter. (To make larger latkes, spoon about 2 tablespoons of the mixture into the pan.) Repeat, adding 2 to 4 more latkes and more oil as needed, but don't crowd the pan. Give yourself room to flip them without breaking any. Reduce the heat to medium and cook until golden, about 2 minutes on each side. With a spatula, transfer the latkes to a plate covered with a paper towel to drain, then transfer to an ovenproof platter and keep warm in a 300°F oven. Add more oil to the pan as needed between batches, giving the oil time to heat before adding the latkes.

To serve, sprinkle with chives or scallions or top with a spoonful of crème fraîche and a chunk of smoked trout.

# Strawberry Arugula Salad

If you start with a spectacular salad, the rest of the meal can be very simple. This one is bright and beautiful, but fast and easy to make. Serve within 5 minutes of mixing the berries and the vinegar, or the berries will be too soft.

$1/4$ cup white balsamic vinegar
 1 teaspoon Dijon mustard or a sweet-hot mustard
$1/2$ cup extra-virgin olive oil
 1 scallion, finely chopped
$1/2$ teaspoon kosher salt
$1/4$ teaspoon freshly cracked black pepper
 1 pint strawberries, cleaned and sliced
$1/2$ pound baby arugula or organic baby greens, washed, dried, and chilled
 2 tablespoons balsamic vinegar to drizzle

Combine the white balsamic vinegar and mustard in a small bowl. Whisk in the olive oil. Whisk in the scallion, salt, and pepper. Add the strawberries to the vinaigrette and marinate for no more than 5 minutes.

Place the greens in a large bowl and spoon in the strawberries with a slotted spoon. Add just enough vinaigrette to barely coat the greens and toss lightly. Arrange on salad plates and drizzle with the 2 tablespoons vinegar. Serve immediately.

OPTION: With Blue Cheese and Hazelnuts

Add $1/4$ cup chopped toasted hazelnuts (see page 24 for toasting tips) and $1/4$ pound of your favorite blue cheese (I like Point Reyes, an artisanal farmstead cheese from northern California; see Resources on page 245). Crumble the cheese evenly over the salads before drizzling with vinegar.

# Orange, Fennel, and Olive Salad

A vibrant combination of juicy oranges, aromatic fennel, and intensely flavorful olives, this is a great salad any time you have vegetarians at the table. (Meat-eaters love it too.) I also serve it with lamb chops instead of the Asparagus-Feta Salsa Verde on page 38.

A mandoline makes quick work of slicing the oranges and the fennel, but if you don't have one, follow the simple directions below. You can easily make more or less of this salad depending on the number of people you're serving: just allow one orange per person.

If your grocery store has an olive bar, look for pitted kalamatas. To pit the olives yourself, you have two options. For a neatly halved olive, make an incision all the way around the olive lengthwise with a small paring knife. Gently twist apart the olive halves and discard the pit. The faster pitting method is to press down on the olive with the flat of a large knife blade. Apply slow pressure until the olive splits or the pit comes to the surface. Then cut the olive in half. You'll feel the knife edge gently hit the pit, which will pop right out.

4 large navel oranges
1 medium fennel bulb or 2 baby fennel bulbs
2 shallots, finely diced or cut into thin slices
6–8 kalamata olives, pitted and halved (see headnote)

$1/4$ cup extra-virgin olive oil
$1 1/2$ tablespoons fresh lemon juice
1 teaspoon sea salt
$1/2$ teaspoon freshly cracked black pepper

## Cat's Note
Cracked pepper adds more intense sparks of flavor than ground pepper. You can crack peppercorns by wrapping them in a few layers of plastic wrap and pounding them on a cutting board with a tenderizing mallet or a hammer.

Peel the oranges and cut each orange in half along its equator, then cut into quarters. (I like to do this in a big wooden bowl to catch all the juice.) Cut thin slices of each quarter—each piece of orange in the salad will be a quarter of an orange wheel. Reserve juice to toss into the salad.

Wash the fennel and remove the green

stalks and any bruised or discolored outer leaves. With a chef's knife, slice across the bulb as thinly as possible, or use a mandoline. Add the fennel slices to the bowl with the orange segments. Add the shallots and olives to the bowl.

In a separate bowl, whisk together the olive oil, lemon juice, and salt. When you're ready to serve the salad, pour the dressing over the orange mixture and toss gently. Transfer the salad to a colorful serving bowl or platter. Sprinkle the salad with cracked pepper.

# Tomato and Shellfish Soup

This is Greek fisherman's soup, which my family on the Greek island of Skopelos would make with whatever shellfish came in on the boat that day. You might not have a fishing boat loaded with shellfish at your disposal, but don't let that stop you. Provided you add 1 to 1½ pounds of shellfish, you can use any combination you like—shrimp and mussels, mussels and clams, or all three—as long as they're fresh. A simple but heady mixture of tomatoes, white wine, onion, and garlic lets the seafood shine. This recipe can be easily doubled.

¼ cup extra-virgin olive oil

1 large onion, halved lengthwise and sliced into half-moons

2 garlic cloves, minced

1 cup dry white wine

1 15-ounce can diced tomatoes

1 tablespoon chopped fresh marjoram, or 1 teaspoon dried

1 tablespoon chopped fresh flat-leaf parsley

2 cups fish stock (page 236) or bottled clam broth or cold water

1–1½ pounds clams, mussels (see note below), and/or shrimp, shelled and deveined

1 teaspoon kosher salt

½ teaspoon freshly ground black pepper

4 thick slices rustic bread, toasted (optional)

Pour the olive oil into a large saucepan over medium-high heat. When the oil is hot but not smoking, add the onion slices and cook until lightly browned, 5 to 7 minutes. Add the garlic, sauté for 2 to 3 minutes more, then pour in the wine. Reduce the heat slightly and simmer for 3 to 4 minutes. Add the tomatoes and the herbs.

Pour in the stock and add the clams and the mussels. As soon as the shells open, 3 to 4 minutes, add the shrimp and simmer just until they are pink, 2 to 3 minutes. Discard any unopened clams and mussels.

Add salt and pepper and serve hot. If you like, add a toasted slice of rustic bread beside each serving.

## Cat's Note

To clean clams, scrub them. Encourage them to purge sand or grit by pouring cold water into a bowl with a teaspoon or two of salt. Add the clams and let them sit for 2 to 3 minutes, then pour out the water, add fresh water and salt, and let them sit for another 2 to 3 minutes. Repeat 2 or 3 times.

Buy mussels the day you plan to use them. About 1 hour before cooking, scrub them with a brush (no soap!) under cold running water to get rid of grit, and pull off the fringed byssus (also called a beard) or scrape it off with a knife. Discard any that are cracked.

# Parmesan, Prosciutto, and Arugula Sandwich

If you make only one recipe from this chapter, this should be it. It's fast and easy *and* luxurious and satisfying. For me, it's a fallback dinner—something I can make much faster than the time it takes to have a pizza delivered. It's also perfect picnic food, packed in a basket with a bottle of wine, and terrific at a tailgating party or as an appetizer.

If you leave out the truffle oil, the sandwich will still be delicious, but it won't have the same flair.

Long, flat ciabatta loaves can be hollowed out quite easily. Before I start layering, I divide the ingredients into two equal amounts, so neither sandwich is shortchanged.

2 ciabatta loaves, 12–14 inches long

2 tablespoons top-quality extra-virgin olive oil

8 ounces prosciutto, thinly sliced

1½ cups baby arugula

6 ounces Parmesan cheese, thinly sliced or shaved

2 tablespoons truffle oil

Cut the ciabatta loaves in half lengthwise. With a big spoon or your fingers, hollow out both halves of each loaf, leaving a shell approximately 1 inch thick. (Stash the ciabatta innards in a resealable plastic bag in your freezer and use them when you need bread crumbs.) With a brush, very lightly coat the insides of the hollowed-out loaves with olive oil. If you don't have a brush, pour the oil into a small bowl and use a spoon to dribble it onto the bread.

Layer half of the prosciutto, arugula, and cheese in each hollowed-out loaf. With a spoon, drizzle the truffle oil over the meat, greens, and cheese. Replace the top half of each loaf and slice into rectangular sandwiches, each about 2 inches wide. Serve or wrap each loaf in foil for a picnic.

# Greek Lamb and Olive Burgers with Garlic "Sauce"

The incredible texture of this juicy, flavorful burger comes from a mix of lamb, chopped kalamata olives, and feta cheese. The garlic "sauce"—a simple combination of yogurt and minced garlic—makes it look as if you've spent some time in the kitchen, when really you're in and out in a flash. You can double or triple this recipe easily when serving a crowd at a barbecue.

If you'd like the sauce to be thick, strain the yogurt through cheesecloth for 30 minutes and discard the liquid before adding the garlic, or use a fine-mesh strainer set over a bowl or a cup.

1 pound ground lamb
$^1/_3$ cup chopped kalamata olives (see pitting tip, page 12)
3 tablespoons dried bread crumbs, preferably panko
2 tablespoons finely chopped onion
1 tablespoon chopped scallions
$^1/_4$ teaspoon kosher salt
$^1/_8$ teaspoon freshly ground black pepper
1 teaspoon chopped fresh oregano
2 tablespoons crumbled feta cheese

GARLIC SAUCE
$^1/_4$ cup plain yogurt
2 garlic cloves, minced

4 onion hamburger rolls, split and toasted
4 lettuce leaves, washed and dried
4 tomato slices
4 cucumber slices (optional)
4 thin slices red onion (optional)

With your hands or a wooden spoon, mix the lamb, olives, bread crumbs, onion, scallions, salt, pepper, oregano, and feta until all the ingredients are evenly distributed. Shape the meat mixture into four $^1/_2$-inch-thick patties.

Preheat a grill or a grill pan. Grill the meat patties over medium-hot coals or pan-grill over medium-high heat for 5 minutes per side. The burgers should no longer be pink in the center.

Cat's Note  I keep panko bread crumbs in my pantry. Panko are Japanese bread crumbs made from the soft center of a bread loaf and look more like flakes than the softer, rounder homemade bread crumbs. Whether you use panko or ordinary dried bread crumbs, they help keep burgers and meat loaf moist and tender.

FOR THE GARLIC SAUCE: While the burgers cook, stir together the yogurt and garlic.

Place each burger on the bottom of a roll, spoon on a little garlic sauce, and top with lettuce, tomato, and cucumber and onion, if using. Cover with the top half of the roll and serve.

# Over-the-Top Ahi Tuna Salad

Top-grade tuna is expensive, but if you want to put together a great meal quickly, you can't do better than ahi. Also called yellowfin, ahi is tender without being oily. It's my first choice for this salad, but you can go with any high-quality tuna: freshness is everything.

This salad is even tastier if you make it the night before, as the tuna absorbs the dressing and the flavors meld. Serve in a bowl or on a platter lined with a broad-leaf lettuce, such as red romaine.

2 tablespoons extra-virgin olive oil
1 pound ahi tuna
30 cherry tomatoes, halved
1 celery rib, finely chopped (about 3/4 cup)
1 small red onion, finely chopped (about 1 cup)
2 scallions, finely chopped
2 tablespoons drained capers
1 teaspoon crushed red pepper flakes
6–8 lettuce leaves for garnish (optional)
2 teaspoons finely chopped fresh flat-leaf parsley

DRESSING

3 tablespoons extra-virgin olive oil
1 tablespoon fresh lemon juice
1 tablespoon red wine vinegar
2 teaspoons chopped fresh oregano
2 large garlic cloves, minced
1/2 teaspoon kosher salt
Freshly ground black pepper

Pour olive oil into a large, heavy skillet and set over high heat. Tilt the pan slightly so that the oil heats evenly and coats the pan bottom. When the oil is almost smoking, carefully place the tuna in the pan and sear on each side until golden brown, about 1 minute. Don't overcook. Transfer the tuna to a plate and let it cool for about 10 minutes. Wrap and refrigerate the tuna if you don't plan to mix the salad right away.

FOR THE DRESSING: In a small bowl, whisk together all the ingredients. Set aside.

Cat's Note  If you're rushed, don't bother dicing the fish. Just cut steak into individual portions, top with the dressing, place some greens next to the fish, and serve.

When the tuna has cooled, dice into bite-sized pieces. In a large bowl, gently toss the tuna with the remaining ingredients except the lettuce and parsley.

Just before serving, pour the dressing over the tuna mixture and mix very gently. If you like, spoon the tuna into a bowl or platter lined with lettuce leaves. Sprinkle with the parsley.

Serve the salad immediately, or refrigerate and serve the next day.

# Spicy Chicken and Peach (or Mango) Stir-Fry

Feel free to use the veggies you have on hand in this stir-fry. If you don't like broccoli, just add more carrot slices, strips of red bell pepper, or some canned water chestnuts. Try using canned pineapple chunks (just a few) in place of the fresh peaches or mangoes. Anything goes: this is definitely cooking from the hip.

I love the zing and the color that fresh peaches or mangoes add, and I like to cut the fruit in a big wooden bowl to save all those great juices. Stirred into the pan at the last minute, they add lots of flavor to the sauce.

The one thing to watch is the amount you have in the pan. A stir-fry cooks quickly, but if your pan is overfilled, cooking slows way down. I often double or triple this recipe, but when cooking it, I stir-fry in two or three batches.

Cut up the chicken the day before and marinate it overnight for better flavor. If you peel and slice the veggies the night before and wrap them tightly in plastic wrap, you can have dinner ready in less than 30 minutes the next day.

MARINADE

2–3 Thai or serrano chilies

¼ cup soy sauce

1 teaspoon minced fresh ginger

2 large garlic cloves, minced

1 pound boneless, skinless chicken breasts, sliced into ½-inch-thick strips

STIR-FRY

1 tablespoon all-purpose flour or cornstarch

1 tablespoon sesame oil or vegetable oil

1 medium onion, diced

1 large carrot, peeled and thinly sliced on the bias

1 cup broccoli florets

½ cup snow peas, strings removed

3 peaches, halved, pitted, and sliced, or 3 mangoes, peeled, pitted, and sliced (see page 61), any juices reserved

Soy sauce, if needed

1 tablespoon coarsely chopped fresh cilantro

1 tablespoon chopped scallions

1 tablespoon slivered almonds, toasted, for garnish

Cat's Note  Toasted slivered almonds improve almost any stir-fry, and toasting the nuts intensifies their flavor. To toast the nuts, toss a few tablespoonfuls into a small, dry skillet and toast over medium heat, stirring, or (my preference) spread them on a baking sheet and toast in a 350°F oven for 2 to 3 minutes. When you can smell their aroma, they're done. Remove the nuts from the hot pan so they don't burn.

FOR THE MARINADE: With a sharp knife, cut the Thai chili in half lengthwise. Seed by scraping the inside of each chili half with your knife. Thinly slice the chili. (Be very careful not to touch your face or eyes while you're working with the chili. As soon as it is sliced, wash your hands and the knife carefully.)

In a medium Pyrex dish or bowl, combine the soy sauce, ginger, garlic, and chili slices. Add the strips of chicken and stir to coat. Cover and refrigerate.

FOR THE STIR-FRY: Sift the flour into a small bowl and set aside. (If using cornstarch, you don't need to sift it.) Heat the oil in a wok or large skillet set over high heat. When the oil is hot, add the onion, stir for 1 to 2 minutes, then add the chicken strips, lifting them out of the marinade with a slotted spoon. Sauté quickly just until the chicken begins to brown and then pour in the marinade. Add the carrot slices and broccoli and lower the heat to medium-high, covering the pan with a lid to keep liquids from evaporating. Cook for 2 to 3 minutes, or until the carrots are tender. Toss in the snow peas and the peach or mango slices and their juices and cook for 2 to 3 minutes. If there doesn't seem to be much liquid in the pan, add 1 to 2 tablespoons soy sauce.

Stir 3 to 4 tablespoons of the pan liquid into the reserved flour or cornstarch, mixing well until completely smooth. Add the mixture to the pan, moving the vegetables to the side with a spatula and stirring the sauce with a small spoon to thicken. Toss in the cilantro and the scallions, give everything one last good stir to mix, and heat it through. Sprinkle with almonds before serving.

## OPTION 1: Vegetarian Stir-Fry

You can make this vegan by leaving out the chicken. Mix the chili, soy sauce, ginger, and garlic and add to the stir-fry with the broccoli and carrots. You can also add tofu cubes, if you like, or extra almonds.

## OPTION 2: With Leftover Chicken

To make this with leftover chicken, pull the meat off the bone, discard the skin and bones, and dice the chicken. Make the marinade, but add it directly to the pan after cooking the onion. Heat the chicken in the marinade for just 1 minute.

# Pork Skewers with Avocado Tzatziki

Marinating pork overnight in a combination of lemon juice, orange juice, and spices makes it succulent. I use boneless center-cut extra-thick pork chops for this dish. If you don't have time to marinate the pork overnight, try to do so for at least 3 hours before grilling (but even if you have only 30 minutes, you'll still get a little tangy flavor).

Threading the skewers with chunks of fresh lemon and orange, with their peels still on, adds a dash of color that complements the pork—and you can squeeze the juice from the grilled fruit over the meat for an extra hit of flavor. (Thread other fruit on the skewers too if you like—try cherry tomatoes or even kumquats.) If the weather isn't cooperating, you can cook the skewers under the broiler.

MARINADE

½ cup plus 3 tablespoons extra-virgin olive oil

¼ cup fresh lemon juice (from 2–3 large lemons)

¼ cup fresh orange juice

½ teaspoon crushed red pepper flakes

1 teaspoon chili powder

2 tablespoons minced garlic

½ teaspoon kosher salt

¼ teaspoon freshly ground black pepper

2 pounds boneless pork, cut into 1½-inch strips or cubes

8–10 8-inch wooden skewers, soaked in cool water for at least 1 hour

3 unpeeled lemons, cut into small wedges

2 unpeeled oranges, cut into small wedges

6 pita rounds, each sliced into 2 half-moons
Iceberg or romaine lettuce, shredded
Avocado Tzatziki (recipe follows)

FOR THE MARINADE: In a large bowl, combine the olive oil, juices, red pepper flakes, chili powder, garlic, salt, and pepper. Add the pork and stir to coat. Cover and refrigerate overnight or for at least 30 minutes.

Preheat the grill.

Thread the skewers with 3 or 4 pieces of marinated pork, alternating with wedges of lemon and orange. Reserve the marinade.

TO GRILL THE PORK: Place the skewers on an area of the grill with no direct flame. Brush with the reserved marinade during the grilling, until the meat is browned on the outside but still slightly pink inside, 4 to 5 minutes per side, or to desired doneness.

TO OVEN-BROIL THE PORK: Set an oven rack about 6 inches from the broiler. Preheat the broiler. Put the skewers on a lightly oiled baking sheet and place under the broiler. After $3^1/_2$ minutes, turn the skewers over and brush with the reserved marinade. Broil for another $3^1/_2$ minutes, brush again with the marinade, and broil for 1 to 2 minutes more, or until meat is browned on the outside but still slightly pink inside.

Serve immediately in pita pockets topped with shredded lettuce and avocado tzatziki.

## Avocado Tzatziki

MAKES 2 TO 3 CUPS

Here's a California twist on a classic Greek condiment. Adding avocado to the tzatziki gives it a richer flavor and color. Excellent with any kind of grilled food, this goes on the table when I serve lamb, chicken, pitas, meatballs, and fried fish. Straining the yogurt through cheesecloth for 30 minutes and discarding the liquid will make it thicker, but you can skip this step.

2 cups plain yogurt (see above)
$^1/_2$ cup extra-virgin olive oil
1 tablespoon fresh lemon juice
1 teaspoon minced garlic

1 teaspoon kosher salt
1 cup peeled, seeded, and grated cucumber
  (1 large cucumber)
1 avocado, peeled and diced

In a medium bowl, stir together the yogurt, olive oil, lemon juice, garlic, and salt. Add the grated cucumber and the diced avocado and mix well. Refrigerate, preferably for at least 1 hour, before serving.

# Creamy Fettuccine with Sausage, Olives, and Broccoli Rabe

SERVES 4

Incredibly easy to make, this is a "wow!" pasta, because every ingredient packs a big hit of flavor. Buy pitted kalamata olives if you can, or pit them yourself (see headnote on page 12).

3 tablespoons extra-virgin olive oil

1 pound hot Italian sausage or fennel sausage, cut into $1/2$-inch slices

4–6 garlic cloves, minced (about 2 tablespoons)

$1/4$ pound broccoli rabe, cleaned and coarsely chopped

Salt

1 pound fettuccine (fresh or dried)

$1/2$ cup pitted kalamata olives (about $1/4$ pound)

$1/4$ cup heavy cream

1 teaspoon crushed red pepper flakes

2 teaspoons chopped fresh oregano (see note)

Freshly ground black pepper

Put water on to boil in a large pot or in a pasta pot fitted with a strainer.

Pour the olive oil into a skillet and set over medium heat. Cook the sausage just until it begins to brown, about 3 minutes. Add the garlic and cook just until fragrant and beginning to brown, about 2 minutes. Add the broccoli rabe and sauté for 3 to 4 minutes.

When the water in the pot is boiling, salt the water, add the pasta, and cook until al dente, about 5 minutes for fresh fettuccine or 8 to 10 minutes for dried.

Add the olives to the skillet. Sauté for 1 minute, then stir in the cream. Drain the pasta and transfer to a large bowl. Add the sausage mixture and toss. Add the red pepper flakes, oregano, and salt and pepper to taste. Toss and serve.

Cat's Note  When using fresh oregano or any herb with thick or woody stems, I pull the leaves off the stems first and chop them.

# Pantry Makeover: Oils

When you're cooking from the hip, the oils in your cabinet must be fresh, lively, and varied. Here's what you'll find in my kitchen.

## Extra-Virgin Olive Oil: 2 to 6 bottles

Olive oils are like wine—you need to taste them to find your favorite. You'll need at least two bottles of olive oil, one that's tasty but less expensive—for pouring into the pan for sautéing—and another that costs more but gives you really terrific flavor when drizzled over fresh tomatoes or even a dessert.

For my cooking oil, I like the traditional oil from Greece called Liohori. It comes in a big tin; I pour it into smaller, dark-tinted bottles that fit into my cupboard. For my everyday oils, I use Apollo, Colavita, and Bertolli. I'm a big fan of DaVero olive oil from the Napa Valley. For my "final drizzle" oil, I like Manni olive oils from Tuscany (see Resources on page 245). Armando Manni makes two oils that are especially smooth and fruity: Per Me (which means "for me") and Per Mio Figlio ("for my child").

Olive oils must be kept in a dark, cool place so they don't turn rancid. (For the same reason, most olive oil bottles are dark green or brown.)

## Vegetable or Canola Oil: 1 bottle

The only consideration for this oil is that it be fresh and neutral-tasting.

## Sesame Oil: 1 small bottle

Sesame oil adds a slightly smoky, nutty flavor to Asian foods and fresh vegetables. Buy sesame oil in small amounts so it does not go rancid.

## Nut Oils: 1 to 3 small bottles

Like sesame oil or truffle oil, nut oils don't stay fresh for long, but they really can make a salad. I like walnut oil to dress green salads, and almond oil is a great choice to dress fruit salads. Store the bottle in a resealable bag in your refrigerator to help keep it fresh longer.

## Truffle Oil: 1 small bottle

Even cooks who spend money on great olive oil see truffle oil as an extravagance, but I don't. A decent, small bottle of truffle oil will set you back nine or ten dollars. That's less than a bottle of wine, and you'll use that truffle oil for twenty to thirty meals.

Truffle oil is a true cooking-from-the-hip ingredient, one that adds more than its cost to the heavenly Parmesan, Prosciutto, and Arugula Sandwich on page 16 or to the orzo on page 45. Store your truffle oil bottle in a resealable plastic bag in the refrigerator to keep it fresh longer.

# Mussels with Saffron Wine Broth and Penne

Saffron and mussels are a classic combination. This sauce is inspired by my time in France. I chop the mussels, so you get a piece in every bite. This technique also releases the juices, which mingle with the saffron broth. You can serve this without the pasta, but you'll want to toast some crusty bread to soak up every drop of the intoxicatingly delicious sauce.

1 large leek, trimmed of all green portions, cleaned, and thinly sliced

½ cup dry white wine

1½ pounds mussels, cleaned (see page 15)

1 garlic clove, minced

1½ cups fish stock (page 236) or bottled clam broth

1 teaspoon kosher salt

6 ounces dried penne (about 2 cups)

Pinch of saffron threads

2 tablespoons chopped fresh flat-leaf parsley

½ teaspoon finely grated lemon zest

Preheat a large skillet with a lid over medium-high heat. Add the leek and the wine and bring to a simmer. Add the mussels and cover the pan. Lift the lid after 2 minutes to check the mussels. Most of the mussels should be open. With tongs, remove opened mussels and set aside in a bowl, because opened mussels will toughen if overcooked. Cover and cook for another minute, then remove any opened mussels and discard any closed mussels. Continue cooking the leek until the liquid has evaporated and the leek is very soft, 1 to 2 minutes. Add the garlic. Cook and stir for 1 minute. Add the fish stock and cook for about 5 minutes, until the liquid is reduced by half.

Meanwhile, bring a large pot of water to a boil. Add the salt and pasta and cook until just tender, about 7 minutes.

While the pasta cooks, remove the mussels from their shells and coarsely chop. Return the mussels to the pan with the leek and add the saffron. When the pasta is al dente, drain. Add the pasta to the mussels, raise the heat to medium-high, and heat for 2 to 3 minutes. The pasta will turn saffron-yellow.

Garnish with the parsley and lemon zest and serve immediately.

Fast

# Saffron

Saffron threads provide a brighter, more intense flavor than saffron powder. The threads are the red stigmas of a crocus that grows throughout the Middle East, India, Greece, and Spain. Saffron is the oldest known spice in use, and it's costly because the stigmas must be gathered from the flowers by hand. It takes only a little bit to flavor a seafood stew, risotto, or even biscuits. If you have saffron powder, use about half the amount given in my recipes, because the powder is concentrated.

In some cases I toss the saffron threads directly into the pot, but most often I let the threads steep in hot water, hot milk, or vinegar to extract the flavor. I crush the saffron threads against a cutting board with the back of a spoon before adding them to the steeping liquid.

# Saffron Honey-Roasted Chicken

SERVES 4 TO 6

1 chicken, 2½–3 pounds
Unsalted butter (about ½ stick)
Kosher salt for sprinkling
About ¼ cup honey
About 2 tablespoons water
½ teaspoon saffron threads

Brushed onto the chicken during the last 10 minutes of roasting, the honey gives just a hint of sweetness to the skin. I've given approximate amounts for the butter and honey, but once you've made this recipe you'll find it's so simple that you won't need to measure the next time.

Preheat the oven to 400°F.

Rinse the chicken and pat dry with paper towels. Place the chicken on a rack in a roasting pan.

Melt the butter in a small saucepan. Drizzle some of the butter over the chicken a little bit at a time, rubbing and turning until the chicken is evenly coated on every side. Don't wash the saucepan. Sprinkle the chicken with salt.

Roast the chicken breast side up for 20 minutes, then turn the chicken and roast for 10 more minutes.

Meanwhile, pour the honey and water into the remaining butter. Add the saffron and heat over low heat until thin enough to brush over the chicken. Turn the chicken breast side up. With a pastry brush or a clean paper towel, brush the honey mixture over the chicken. Roast for another 10 to 15 minutes, or until an instant-read thermometer registers 170°F when inserted into the widest part of the thigh without touching the bone.

Remove the chicken from the oven and let rest for 10 to 15 minutes before carving and serving.

# Lamb Chops with Asparagus-Feta Salsa Verde

How do you transform plain lamb chops into a spectacular meal in a flash? Easy. Make this quick, beautiful salsa from fresh asparagus and feta cheese and serve it over pan-seared chops. The great thing about a salsa verde is that almost anything green goes. Zucchini, celery, and green beans are all good options. Asparagus is my choice. When it's in season, it takes lamb chops from ho-hum to oh, yeah!

To get the maximum flavor and speed up your meal prep, marinate the lamb overnight. But if you're rushed, you can marinate the lamb for as little as 15 minutes, and you'll still have a winner.

¼ cup fresh lemon juice (from 2–3 lemons)
4 tablespoons extra-virgin olive oil
3 tablespoons chopped fresh oregano
1½ teaspoons kosher salt
1 teaspoon freshly ground black pepper

1 pound lamb chops (about 4 shoulder chops or 6–8 rib chops or loin chops)
Asparagus-Feta Salsa Verde (recipe follows)

In a Pyrex baking dish just large enough to hold the lamb chops in a single layer, combine the lemon juice, 3 tablespoons of the olive oil, oregano, salt, and pepper. Place the lamb in the dish and turn to coat the chops with the marinade. Cover and refrigerate while you make the salsa verde. (If you marinate the lamb the night before, that's even better.)

Preheat the oven to 250°F.

Cat's Notes  I like lamb shoulder chops, which give you the best value for your money.

If you find pencil-sized, extra-tender young asparagus, you don't need to cook it. Just slice the stalks thinly on the bias, coat with a tablespoon of olive oil, and season with salt and freshly ground black pepper to taste before you mix with the other salsa ingredients.

In a large skillet, heat the remaining 1 tablespoon olive oil over high heat until almost smoking. Remove the chops from the marinade. Sear in 2 batches on both sides just to brown the chops, then reduce the heat to medium-high and cook for about 4 minutes per side for shoulder chops, 2$\frac{1}{2}$ minutes per side for rib chops, and 1$\frac{1}{2}$ minutes per side for loin chops for medium-rare, adding another 20 to 30 seconds per side for medium-well done.

Place the first batch of chops on an ovenproof platter in the oven to keep warm while you cook the remaining chops.

Remove the chops from the oven and let rest for 3 minutes to allow the juices to be re-absorbed. Spoon the salsa over the chops and serve immediately.

## Asparagus-Feta Salsa Verde

Kosher salt
$\frac{1}{2}$ bunch medium asparagus (6–8 stalks)
$\frac{1}{2}$ cup crumbled feta cheese (3 ounces)
1 tablespoon chopped fresh flat-leaf parsley

1 garlic clove, minced
$\frac{1}{4}$ cup extra-virgin olive oil
2 tablespoons red wine vinegar
Freshly ground black pepper

Fill a medium saucepan with water, add a scant tablespoon of salt, and bring to a boil over high heat. Fill a large bowl with ice water.

While the water is heating, snap off the tough ends of the asparagus and peel the stems (if your asparagus is fairly tender, you can skip peeling the ends). When the water reaches a boil, add the asparagus to the pot. Cook until the spears are slightly tender and bright green, 4 to 6 minutes. If you have thin, tender asparagus, cook for just 1 to 2 minutes. Don't overcook. Use tongs to transfer the asparagus to the bowl of ice water. As soon as they're cool, remove the spears from the water, place on a plate covered with a clean dish towel or paper towels, and gently pat dry.

Slice the asparagus spears on the bias into 1$\frac{1}{2}$-inch pieces. In a medium bowl, toss together the asparagus, feta, parsley, garlic, olive oil, and vinegar. Season with salt and pepper to taste.

# Pan-Seared Filet of Beef
# with Corn Basil Succotash

SERVES 4

Basil and beef stock give this succotash a new flair. If you want to make this recipe without the beef stock, see the option below and make a light broth from the corn cobs after you slice off all the kernels.

Of course, fresh is always best, but when you're making the beef stock version, you can use frozen corn kernels if you're short on time.

4 ears corn, shucked and cleaned

4 6-ounce beef filets

1 teaspoon kosher salt

1/2 teaspoon freshly ground black pepper

2 tablespoons extra-virgin olive oil

1/4 cup grated pecorino cheese

1 teaspoon unsalted butter

2 medium tomatoes, finely diced

1 small onion, finely chopped

1 scallion, chopped

1 cup beef stock, homemade (page 237) or store-bought

2 tablespoons chopped fresh basil

With a long, sharp knife, carefully cut the corn kernels from the cobs. Set aside.

Preheat the oven to 400°F.

Season the beef with the salt and the pepper. In a large skillet over medium-high heat, heat the olive oil and sear the beef on all sides, just until brown and caramelized. Place the filets on an ovenproof platter, top each filet with 1 tablespoon of the cheese, and put in the oven for 4 to 5 minutes.

Heat the butter in the same skillet over medium-high heat. When it's foamy, add the corn, tomatoes, onion, and scallion. Pour in the stock and add the basil. Reduce the heat and simmer for 3 to 4 minutes, or until the vegetables taste done and moist but are no longer soupy.

Ladle the succotash into four individual bowls, top each with one of the filets, and serve.

OPTION: Corn Cob Broth

You can make a very light, fresh-tasting corn broth from the cobs after you've sliced off all the kernels. Put the cobs in a medium saucepan and add enough cold water to cover them. Simmer for 10 to 15 minutes.

Add kosher salt and freshly ground black pepper to taste.

# Curried Broccoli Salad

SERVES 6 TO 8

If you like curried chicken salad, you'll love curried broccoli salad. My grandmother made this salad for every family reunion, and now my mom makes it. It's a good way to get kids to give broccoli a second look. For a lighter version made with olive oil instead of mayonnaise, see Option 1 at the end of this recipe. If you like, you can prepare this the night before, since the flavors just get better.

2 tablespoons kosher salt
2 pounds broccoli florets (from about
    3 bunches broccoli)
1/2 pound pancetta or strips of thick-sliced
    bacon
1 cup chopped pecans (toast before
    chopping, if desired; see page 24)
1 cup raisins
1/2 cup hulled sunflower seeds
1 medium red onion, finely chopped

DRESSING
1 cup mayonnaise
1 tablespoon Madras curry powder
1/4 cup sugar
1/4 cup rice wine vinegar
1/2 teaspoon sea salt
1/8 teaspoon freshly ground black pepper

Fill a large pot with water and put it over high heat to boil. Fill a large bowl or your sink with ice and cold water.

When the water boils, add the salt and the broccoli. Cook for 1 to 2 minutes, or until the broccoli is bright green and still somewhat firm, barely tender enough to pierce with a knife. Use a long-handled strainer or tongs to transfer the broccoli to the ice-water bath. After 2 to 3 minutes, remove the broccoli from the ice water and place in a colander to drain. Line a bowl with paper towels, transfer the broccoli to the bowl, and refrigerate it while you cook the pancetta.

Dice the pancetta. In a large skillet over medium-high heat, sear the pancetta, stirring, until the pieces are crisp and browned. Remove the pancetta from the pan and allow it to drain on paper towels.

Remove the broccoli from the refrigerator and chop coarsely. Place in a large serving bowl with the pancetta, pecans, raisins, sunflower seeds, and red onion.

FOR THE DRESSING: Whisk together all the ingredients in a medium bowl.

Add the dressing to the salad, toss gently, and serve.

## OPTION 1: Without the Mayo

In this version, dried currants replace the raisins, olive oil is used instead of the mayonnaise, and the amount of curry powder is reduced.

DRESSING

¼ cup plus 2 tablespoons rice wine vinegar

1½ tablespoons sugar

2 teaspoons Madras curry powder

¼ teaspoon kosher salt

Freshly ground black pepper

½ cup extra-virgin olive oil

In a large bowl, mix the vinegar and the sugar together until the sugar is dissolved. Whisk in the curry powder, the salt, and pepper to taste. Continue whisking and very slowly drizzle the olive oil into the vinegar mixture until all the oil is incorporated. Taste and add more salt and pepper, if desired, then set the dressing aside and prepare the broccoli and the pancetta, following the instructions above. Use 1 cup dried currants in place of the raisins.

Pour the dressing evenly over the salad, tossing lightly to mix thoroughly. Chill for 1 to 2 hours before serving.

## OPTION 2: Vegetarian

Leave out the pancetta.

## OPTION 3: Vegan

Follow the instructions in Option 1 and leave out the pancetta.

# Three-Bean Salad with Fresh Mint

Three-bean salad is an old-fashioned standby, and you probably already have the main ingredients in your pantry or freezer. There's nothing old-fashioned about the taste of this one, though. I've given it a bit of a Greek spin with sherry vinegar, lots of lemon zest, and fresh herbs (mint in this case, but use what you have). For the sweetest flavor, slice the red onion very thin. This hearty salad is a good picnic staple, easy to pack up and take along.

1 small red onion, quartered and thinly sliced

1 8-ounce package frozen green beans, thawed

1 15-ounce can chickpeas, drained

1 15-ounce can kidney beans, drained

2 tablespoons finely chopped fresh mint

2 teaspoons finely grated lemon zest

1/4 cup sherry vinegar

1/4 cup top-quality extra-virgin olive oil

1 tablespoon sugar

1 teaspoon kosher salt

1/4 teaspoon freshly ground black pepper

Place the onion in a large bowl, and add the remaining ingredients. Stir and taste, and add more lemon zest, mint, salt, or pepper, if you like. Serve or refrigerate until ready to serve.

# Two-Bean Salad with Hearts of Palm and Blue Cheese

SERVES 6 TO 8

This is a dressed-up version of the bean salad on page 43, and the only ingredient that may be new to you is hearts of palm, which most grocery stores carry in cans or jars. This salad couldn't be easier to put together. If you have a large, clear serving bowl, use it to show off the salad's layers.

VINAIGRETTE
1 tablespoon Dijon mustard
1/2 cup sherry vinegar
1 teaspoon sea salt
1/2 cup extra-virgin olive oil
1/4 cup chopped shallots

1 8-ounce can hearts of palm, drained
1 cup drained kidney beans
1 cup diced cucumber
1 cup halved cherry tomatoes or sliced
  regular tomatoes
1 cup drained chickpeas
1 cup baby arugula leaves
1 cup crumbled blue cheese

FOR THE VINAIGRETTE: In a small bowl, whisk together all the ingredients. Set aside.

Slice the hearts of palm into rings and set aside. In a small bowl, combine the kidney beans and 2 tablespoons of the vinaigrette. Toss quickly to flavor the beans, then spoon the beans into a large serving bowl to form the salad's bottom layer. Using the same small bowl, toss the cucumber with a little vinaigrette, and add to the serving bowl to form the next layer. Follow the same steps with the tomatoes, chickpeas, arugula, and the hearts of palm. Finish by sprinkling the cheese over the salad. Chill, preferably for 1 hour, and serve.

# Orzo with Asiago Cheese

Very rich and satisfying yet simple to make, this orzo is a good side dish for the Lamb Chops with Asparagus-Feta Salsa Verde (page 37) or with any grilled beef, chicken, or pork. See page 30 for tips on storing truffle oil. And if you don't have truffle oil, go on and serve the orzo without it; the Asiago cheese provides plenty of flavor.

1 tablespoon plus 1 teaspoon kosher salt

1 1/3 cups orzo

1 tablespoon unsalted butter

1/2 cup plus 3 tablespoons grated Asiago cheese

1 teaspoon truffle oil

1/2 teaspoon freshly ground black pepper

Bring 4 quarts of water to a boil in a large pot. Add the 1 tablespoon salt and the orzo and cook for 5 to 7 minutes, or until the pasta is al dente. Drain the orzo.

In a 10-inch skillet, melt the butter over medium heat. Add the orzo and 3 tablespoons of the cheese. Drizzle on the truffle oil and sprinkle with the remaining 1 teaspoon salt and pepper. Toss well. Spoon the orzo into a serving bowl, top with the remaining 1/2 cup cheese, and serve immediately.

## Cat's Note
To make this vegan, omit the cheese and butter and check the label of the orzo to be sure it's just semolina flour and water, with no eggs added. Cook and drain the orzo and spoon it into a serving bowl. Drizzle the orzo with the truffle oil and sprinkle it with the 1 teaspoon salt and the pepper. Toss well and serve.

# Chocolate Brownie Cupcakes

These cupcakes can swing both ways: not only do they please kids, but they can be dressed up for adult tastes by using a high-quality chocolate, such as Valrhona, Callebaut, El Rey, or Scharffen Berger (see Resources, page 245).

2 1/2 ounces unsweetened chocolate, coarsely chopped

3/4 cup plus 3 tablespoons cake flour

1/2 teaspoon baking powder

1/4 teaspoon salt

7 tablespoons (3/4 stick plus 1 tablespoon) unsalted butter, softened

1 1/4 cups sugar

2 large eggs

1/2 cup chopped walnuts

1 1/4 teaspoons vanilla extract

Seven-Minute Frosting (page 48), Peanut Butter Frosting (page 48), or Honey Frosting (page 48)

Place a rack in the middle of the oven and preheat the oven to 350°F. Line a standard (1/3-cup) muffin pan with 12 paper cupcake liners.

Place the chocolate in the top of a double boiler. (If you don't have a double boiler, use a wide stainless-steel bowl that fits snugly over a saucepan one third full of water.) The water should be hot but not boiling. Stir the chocolate every minute or so until it's melted, then remove the pan from the heat and set aside to cool.

Sift the flour, baking powder, and salt onto a piece of wax paper; set aside.

Place the butter and the sugar in a large bowl and, using a hand mixer, thoroughly cream together until light and fluffy. Crack the eggs one at a time into a small bowl to prevent any shell from getting into the sugar mixture, beat lightly, then gradually add to the sugar mixture, beating well after each addition. Add the cooled chocolate and blend thoroughly. Add the sifted dry ingredients a little at a time, beating at medium speed after each addition. After adding the last of the flour mixture, beat until smooth. Stir in the nuts and vanilla extract.

Spoon the batter into the muffin cups and bake for 20 to 22 minutes, or until a toothpick inserted in the center comes out clean.

Transfer the cupcakes to a wire rack and allow them to cool completely before icing.

# Seven-Minute Frosting

I love this frosting because it's delicious and really holds up—even through the next day.

| | |
|---|---|
| 2 large egg whites | 1 tablespoon light corn syrup |
| 1 1/2 cups sugar | 1/2 teaspoon salt |
| 1/2 cup water | 1 teaspoon vanilla extract |

Pour 2 inches of water into the bottom of a double boiler and bring it to a simmer over high heat. In the top of the double boiler, off the heat, combine all the ingredients except the vanilla. (If you don't have a double boiler, use a wide stainless-steel bowl that fits snugly over a saucepan one third full of water.) Beat the mixture with a hand mixer on low for about 1 minute to blend thoroughly. Place the bowl over the simmering water, reduce the heat to medium, and beat constantly with the mixer on medium-high for 7 minutes, or until the frosting stands in stiff peaks and has tripled in volume. Lift the pan off the water and beat on high vigorously for 2 to 3 minutes more, until the frosting has cooled and is thick and glossy. Beat in the vanilla.

### OPTION 1: Peanut Butter Frosting

Place 1 cup of the frosting in a medium bowl and whisk in 1/2 cup smooth peanut butter. Fold in the rest of the frosting gently, using a rubber spatula.

### OPTION 2: Honey Frosting

Reduce the sugar to 1 cup and add 1/2 cup honey when you combine the ingredients. I like lavender honey, but you can use orange blossom honey or whatever variety you've got in the pantry. You may need to beat the honey frosting for an additional minute to get the egg whites to stand in stiff peaks. If you like, you can add a few drops of rose water to give the frosting just a hint of rose. (You'll find sources for great honeys and rose water on page 245.)

# Mildred's Date Bars

When my mother, Virginia, makes these soft, cakelike bars, the whole house takes on the rich smell of sweet, warm dates. My mom lived on a farm in Illinois when she was a girl, and the Stallman family owned the next farm over. Mildred Stallman gave the recipe for these date bars to my grandmother and advised her to hide the bars until her Christmas tins were filled, because if the kids got hold of the bars, they'd polish them off. (That was true fifty years ago, and it's still true today.) When my grandmother made these bars for us, she coated them with powdered sugar, which made it hard to sneak them—but she'd always put a few bars aside so that my brothers and I would get one last taste of this treat on the long drive home after Christmas.

The recipe calls for finely chopped dates, but dates are sticky, so just chop them as best you can.

1 cup sugar

3 large eggs

1 cup all-purpose flour

1 teaspoon baking powder

1 cup chopped walnuts

1 cup finely chopped dates

Confectioners' sugar for sprinkling (about ¼ cup)

Place the rack in the middle of the oven and preheat the oven to 350°F.

Beat the sugar and eggs together in a large bowl with a hand mixer until light and fluffy. Add the flour and baking powder and beat well. Add the nuts and dates and mix thoroughly. Pour the batter into an ungreased 9-by-13-inch baking pan.

Bake for about 25 minutes, or until a toothpick inserted into the center comes out clean and the top is golden brown. Let cool in the pan for 15 to 20 minutes. (Set the pan on a wire rack if you'd like it to cool a little faster.) Cut into 48 bars. Sift the confectioners' sugar onto a large piece of parchment or wax paper and transfer the bars onto the sugar, using a spatula. Sift more confectioners' sugar over the tops to coat the bars completely.

Stored in an airtight container, these bars stay moist and soft for a week.

The kids are running through the kitchen, the doorbell is ringing, and the phone won't stop. These recipes let you step away for a minute and come back without worrying that you'll lose your place or compromise your results.

## Appetizers

Sun-Dried Tomato Crostini   53

Leek and Onion Tartlets   55

Shiitake Duxelles Tea Sandwiches   56

COOKING WITHOUT MEASURING: Watermelon, Lime, Cashews, and Coconut   57

Shrimp and Scallop Coconut Seviche   60

## Soups and Salads

Chickpea and Roasted Pepper Soup   63

Watermelon Gazpacho   64

Charred Eggplant-Tomato Soup with Cilantro   66

Endive, Honeydew, and Pear Salad with Honey Dressing   68

## Main Dishes

Asian Steak and Spinach Salad   72

Salmon-Topped Hash   74

Lettuce "Gyros" Filled with Spicy Halibut with Feta-Mint Tzatziki   78

Thai Chicken Salad with Cabbage   83

Curried Red Snapper   85

Grilled Skirt Steak with Shiitake Mushroom Salsa   86

Pasta with Roasted Pepper and Tomato Sauce   88

Farfalle and Herb Salad with Peas   91

## Side Dishes

White Cheddar Corn Bread with Scallions   92

Curried Lentils with Butternut Squash   93

COOKING WITHOUT MEASURING: Roasted Sweet Potatoes with Rosemary and Orange   94

## Desserts

Rizogalo (Creamy Rice Pudding)   95

Cherry Clafouti   97

# Easy

# Sun-Dried Tomato Crostini

SERVES 4 TO 6

Start with intensely flavorful ingredients—such as sun-dried tomatoes and goat cheese—and you'll have great-tasting crostini in a heartbeat. I consider sun-dried tomatoes a pantry essential and stock up on them when I see them at a farmers' market, but the packets in grocery stores work too. Look for tomatoes that have a slightly moist appearance; don't buy them if they look dry or broken.

You can go in lots of directions with this recipe. Instead of sun-dried tomatoes, try Roasted Cherry Tomatoes (page 241) or Slow-Cooked Figs (page 243).

About ½ baguette, cut into twelve ¼-inch-thick slices
1 tablespoon extra-virgin olive oil
1 small onion, finely chopped

½ cup chopped sun-dried tomatoes
1 teaspoon chopped fresh thyme
½ teaspoon kosher salt
2–3 tablespoons soft fresh goat cheese

Preheat the oven to 350°F.

Arrange the bread slices in a single layer on a baking sheet and bake for 6 to 8 minutes until toasted.

In a small skillet, heat the olive oil on medium-high heat. Sauté the onion until golden brown, 5 to 7 minutes. Add the tomatoes, thyme, and salt and sauté for 2 minutes to bring out the flavor of the tomatoes. Pour onto a plate to cool and set aside.

## Cat's Note

Crostini is a great use for day-old baguettes.

Spread the cheese lightly over the crostini. When the onion-tomato mixture has cooled slightly, spoon about ½ tablespoon onto each crostini. Serve warm or at room temperature.

Easy

# Grown-Up Time
# The New Happy Hour

When my son, Zoran, was born, I left a job that I loved, as executive chef at Postino, a restaurant in northern California. I was ready for the nighttime feedings, ready for the *Goodnight Moon* readings, but it took some time to adjust to evenings with a toddler. At Postino, I could handle 300 dinners a night—in fact, I loved the fast pace and the way the kitchen staff seemed almost choreographed. In my new life, I'd come home from a day of filming a cooking segment or teaching a class, ready just to kick back with my family and a glass of wine. Instead I'd be faced with making dinner and an evening that was somehow more tiring than the craziest nights at Postino.

It took our next-door neighbors, Alan and Barbara, to change things. They'd appear at our door at six p.m., Barbara holding a bottle of wine and two wineglasses and Alan holding one perfectly made martini. "We're coming to bug you," Barbara would say, hugging both of us, setting down the wine, and picking up Zoran, who would hold up his arms to her. She didn't ask, "May we come in?" or "Is this a good time?"—which was good, because I would have sent them away so that I could vacuum the rug and pick up Zoran's toys. Instead I let them in and got just what I needed: a glass of wine with two good-humored people who took turns holding my baby.

Bars have given the idea of happy hour a bad rap—it's not about the alcohol. It doesn't matter whether your glass holds wine or cranberry juice—the point is to stop. Stop picking up toys. Stop moving ahead to the next task. Take a sip of wine or cranberry juice and a deep breath. Share a laugh with another grown-up.

We all need a decompression period, a time between the workday and the home work to stop rushing. Alan and Barbara never stayed long enough to wear out their welcome, and I realized that evenings starting with their visit were better all the way until bedtime—both for me and for Zoran.

Happy hour can't be an everyday thing. But I try to make time for one or two happy hours a week. And when I prepare any appetizer that seems just right for happy hour, I make extra. This gives us an excuse to drop in on people we like, friends we know are at home with their own kids, facing that long evening. I'll call and say, "We just made these little leek tartlets, and we have too many. We're going to drop them at your house and be out of your hair before dinner." Nobody has ever told me no. And when they open their door, I never ask whether it's a good time. "We're coming to bug you," I say.

# Leek and Onion Tartlets

Buy prebaked miniature phyllo shells from your grocer's freezer and fill them with a basic leek custard. Before you know it, these little tartlets will emerge from your oven looking very black-tie. You don't even need to thaw the shells. Just pull them from your freezer, fill, and pop in the oven.

You can add leftover ham, baby spinach, or salmon to the shells before baking the tartlets—or, my own favorite, fresh crabmeat. You can dress up the tartlets with a dollop of crème fraîche, a spoonful of caviar, and a sprinkling of chives, or top them with whatever you have. But even if you just serve them right from the oven, straight up, they're still a welcome treat.

1 tablespoon unsalted butter
1/2 cup finely chopped well-cleaned leeks
    (white and light green parts only)
1/2 cup finely chopped onion
1 large egg, beaten
1/2 cup light cream

1/4 teaspoon kosher salt
1/8 teaspoon freshly ground black pepper
1/8 teaspoon freshly grated nutmeg
30 prebaked frozen miniature phyllo shells
    (two 15-ounce packages; not thawed)

Place a rack in the middle of the oven and preheat the oven to 350°F.

In a large skillet over medium-low heat, melt the butter. Add the leeks and onion and stir constantly. Cook until soft, 8 to 10 minutes. Remove from the heat and set aside to cool.

In a small bowl, whisk the egg, cream, salt, pepper, and nutmeg together. Stir the cooled onion mixture into the egg mixture. Divide among the tartlet shells. Place the tarts on a baking sheet and bake until the custard sets, 10 to 15 minutes.

Serve the tartlets warm or at room temperature.

OPTION: With Crab

Add just a little fresh crabmeat for a completely different appetizer. Pick over 1/4 cup of lump crabmeat, removing any shells and cartilage, and coarsely chop. Add a scant 1/4 teaspoon crabmeat to each phyllo shell before you spoon in the custard mixture. Bake as directed. Top with crème fraîche, homemade (page 239) or store-bought, and a touch of caviar, if you like.

# Shiitake Duxelles Tea Sandwiches

This classic French preparation of finely diced mushrooms, shallots, and garlic is a great appetizer when you're entertaining or for picnics or brunch. I let the mixture cool, then spread it on thin slices of brioche to make open-faced tea sandwiches. They're small, but they pack a big, bold flavor.

You can substitute any mushrooms you like for the shiitakes. Because the duxelles keeps for several days in the fridge, you can make it ahead. It takes just a minute or two to spread it on the brioche.

DUXELLES

- 2 tablespoons extra-virgin olive oil
- 2 tablespoons finely chopped shallots
- 2 cups minced shiitake mushrooms
- 1 garlic clove, minced
- 1 teaspoon kosher salt
- ¼ teaspoon freshly ground black pepper

- 1 1-pound loaf of brioche or white or wheat bread, crusts removed
- ½ cup Easy Aïoli (page 238), crème fraîche, homemade (page 239) or store-bought, or store-bought mayo whisked with 1 teaspoon fresh lemon juice
- 2 tablespoons finely chopped fresh chives or scallions (green tops only)

Cat's Note  I generally choose small shiitakes because they tend to be cleaner, sweeter, and prettier. Select those with caps that are slightly curled under. The gills should look tight and firm, and if there is a pale-colored filament over the gills, it means the mushroom was allowed to develop slowly, and you can bet its flavor will be intense. The fresher the mushroom, the clearer the flavor.

FOR THE DUXELLES: Pour the olive oil into a large skillet over medium-high heat and, when the oil is hot, add the shallots. Cook for 2 to 3 minutes. Add the mushrooms and cook for 2 minutes, then add the garlic. Continue cooking until the liquid from the mushrooms has evaporated, about 3 more minutes. Add the salt and the pepper and set aside to cool.

Cut the brioche into thin slices. Spread the aïoli onto half of the slices and spoon on a generous tablespoon of the cooled duxelles. Sprinkle with chives and top with the remaining slices of bread. Cut into small finger sandwiches and arrange on a serving platter.

# Watermelon, Lime, Cashews, and Coconut

For each guest, plate either 1 or 2 quarter slices of melon with the rind still on. (I like to cut the whole melon lengthwise, then cut each half lengthwise again, which yields 4 long quarters that can be cut into slices easily.)

On the plate next to each melon slice, add a small pile of chopped cashew nuts, a mound of grated coconut, toasted if you like (see note on page 155), and a juicy lime wedge. You can serve this with knives and forks or let everyone go hands-on.

Instead of nuts and coconut, you can serve the melon slices with chunks of feta cheese and chopped mint leaves or a drizzle of balsamic vinegar, a few thin slices of a spicy salami, and some shavings of Parmesan cheese.

Watermelon doesn't need a whole lot of help to shine. A simple slice on a plate surrounded with condiments makes an easy, awesome presentation, is fun for your guests, and doesn't steal any glory from the melon.

# The Easiest Seafood Possible

If you're the type who sees a recipe for seviche and automatically flips to the next page, hold on for a second! Give this method of "cooking" fish in lemon or lime juice a second chance. I love preparing fish this way, especially on a hot day. I'll give you three reasons to try seviche.

### You can tell when it's done.
People worry that they'll be serving fish that's raw-tasting. Four to ten hours are optimal, so start marinating in the morning for dinnertime or marinate the evening before for a brunch. You can tell just by looking at the seafood whether it's done: if you see any translucence, it's still not ready and should sit in the citrus juice for another hour or two.

### The fish holds up to the citrus juice longer than you'd expect.
Once you remove the seafood from the citrus juice, it can be covered and kept in the fridge for hours and still be firm and delicious and not in the least bit mushy.

### You can quickly precook fish if you want to be absolutely safe.
With seviche I rely on my senses to buy seafood that's fresh and sweet-smelling, and I don't bother precooking it. But if you would rather dip it into boiling water for just a few seconds (no more than 4 seconds), then you can rid yourself of the worry that it isn't cooked and also shorten the time the seafood has to rest in the citrus juice.

# Shrimp and Scallop Coconut Seviche

This is my style of cooking when the weather is hot. Get shrimp and scallops, pour on fresh lime juice, pop it into the fridge in the morning, and by evening the citrus juice has done the work for you.

The trick here is to get super-fresh seafood and to cut it into small chunks so that the lime juice can really penetrate it, then add spicy coconut milk and chunks of mango and serve it all in a coconut shell (available in most large grocery stores). As an appetizer or a salad, this is easy, impressive, and cool, especially when served with ice-cold Sake Margaritas (page 117).

Rock shrimp are best for this dish. Since they generally don't come in a shell, they're easy to prepare. Their size is just right, so you don't need to cut them up before immersing in the juice—and because they're not as sleek as peeled shrimp, they absorb the juice better. Rock shrimp can be hard to find, though, so if you use regular shrimp, just choose the freshest and cut them into ¼-inch chunks or smaller. Choose regular shrimp that are sold in the shell, because the shells keep them fresh longer.

Most important, use your senses when buying seafood for seviche. Scallops should be ivory- or cream-colored, with a translucent quality. Shrimp should look firm and clean, with no black spots or rings. Shellfish should have the briny smell of the sea; never buy shellfish that smells sour or fishy.

¼ pound small to medium shrimp (rock shrimp or regular shrimp), peeled and deveined

¼ pound scallops

⅓–½ cup fresh lime juice, plus 2 tablespoons (from 7–10 large limes for ½ cup juice)

2 tablespoons fresh lemon juice

½ cup unsweetened coconut milk

2 tablespoons extra-virgin olive oil

1 jalapeño pepper, halved and seeded

1 tablespoon chopped fresh cilantro

1 garlic clove, peeled

½ small red onion, thinly sliced

½ teaspoon kosher salt or Citrus-Flavored Salt (page 244)

1 mango, peeled, pitted, and diced (see page 61)

1 coconut, halved (optional)

1 tablespoon unsweetened shredded coconut for garnish (optional)

Warmed tortilla chips for serving

If you're using regular shrimp, you'll need to cook them, and you can cook the scallops too, if you want, though I never do. To cook the seafood, bring a medium pot half full of water to a boil. Fill a large bowl with ice water. With a long-handled strainer or a slotted spoon, dip the shrimp or scallops into the boiling water $1/2$ cup at a time, immersing for just a second or two, then quickly transfer the seafood to the ice water. Remove the shrimp or scallops from the cold water immediately and spread them on a plate lined with a clean dish towel or paper towels.

If the scallops are particularly thick, you may want to slice each one in half horizontally into 2 thinner disks. Cut each scallop or scallop half into 8 wedges. Leave the rock shrimp whole or cut the regular shrimp into chunks that approximately match the size of the scallop wedges.

Put the scallops and the shrimp in a medium bowl and pour about $1/2$ cup lime juice over them, or enough to cover the seafood. Toss so that each piece is given a good lime-juice bath. Cover and place the bowl in the refrigerator to marinate for 4 to 10 hours. The shellfish are done when they are completely white and opaque and don't look or taste raw. Remove from the lime juice and discard the juice.

Meanwhile, in a separate bowl, mix the remaining 2 tablespoons lime juice with the lemon juice, coconut milk, and olive oil. You can chop the jalapeño, cilantro, and garlic by hand, but if you have a food processor, it's much easier to pulse them together. Add the jalapeño mixture to the coconut milk mixture and stir in the red onion. Add the salt and mix well. Refrigerate for several hours or overnight.

In a large bowl, combine the shrimp and scallops and the coconut milk mixture, tossing well. Add the mango chunks and toss gently. Taste and add more salt or fresh lime juice, if desired.

For a knockout presentation, spoon the seviche into the coconut shell halves and sprinkle with unsweetened coconut, if desired. Pile warm tortilla chips around the coconut shells.

# Chickpea and Roasted Pepper Soup

You'd never guess from its sultry taste or bright color that this is a from-the-cupboard-to-the-pot kind of soup. Called *rivithia* in Greece, it's eaten during the long fast before Easter, when meat isn't allowed.

The red pepper strips in a jar work well, so don't spend time roasting peppers if you don't have to.

2 tablespoons extra-virgin olive oil
1 medium onion, finely chopped
1 garlic clove, minced
2 15-ounce cans chickpeas, drained
1 tablespoon finely chopped fresh rosemary
4 cups homemade or store-bought chicken stock or vegetable stock (pages 231–235)

1 bay leaf
1 8-ounce jar roasted peppers, cut into thin strips, or 1 red bell pepper, roasted (page 242), peeled, and seeded
1 teaspoon kosher salt
1/2 teaspoon freshly ground black pepper
4–8 sprigs fresh flat-leaf parsley, chopped, for garnish (optional)

Heat the olive oil in a large saucepan over medium-high heat. Add the onion and sauté, stirring constantly, until lightly browned, 5 to 7 minutes. Add the garlic and sauté for 1 to 2 minutes to soften and bring out the fragrance. Add the chickpeas and rosemary, mixing well.

Pour in the stock, add the bay leaf, and reduce the heat to medium-low.

In a food processor or a blender, puree the contents of the jar of roasted pepper strips (or your own roasted red peppers). Add the red pepper puree to the soup and simmer for about 1 hour. Remove the bay leaf and add the salt and pepper before serving, and top with a sprinkle of parsley, if desired.

# Watermelon Gazpacho ·

People sit up and take notice when you carry this lovely summer soup to the table. The watermelon gives it gorgeous color, and the sweetness of the melon is a perfect counterpoint to the onion, pepper, and lime juice. I like to use a whole jalapeño pepper, but it's smart to start with half a pepper and taste the gazpacho before adding the rest, because jalapeños can vary in intensity. If the weather is extra hot, chill the soup bowls in your freezer until you're ready to serve the gazpacho.

6 cups chopped, seeded watermelon; reserve
    juice
1 cup peeled, seeded, and diced cucumber
1 red bell pepper, diced
1 yellow bell pepper, diced
1/2 jalapeño pepper, seeded and diced
3 celery hearts, diced
1/2 small red onion, finely diced
1/4 cup finely chopped fresh mint

1/4 cup finely chopped fresh flat-leaf parsley
2 tablespoons plus 1 teaspoon lime juice
    (from 2 large limes)
3 tablespoons red wine vinegar
1/2 teaspoon kosher salt
    Freshly ground black pepper
1/4 cup crème fraîche, homemade (page 239)
    or store-bought (optional)

Puree the watermelon and any reserved juice in a blender or food processor until smooth. Set aside.

In a large bowl, toss the cucumber, peppers, celery, onion, herbs, lime juice, vinegar, salt, and pepper to taste. Pour the watermelon puree over the vegetables, cover the bowl with plastic wrap, and refrigerate until well chilled, at least 1 hour.

Taste and season with more salt and black pepper or jalapeño, if it's not spicy enough. Serve very cold, topped with a spoonful of crème fraîche, if you like.

# Charred Eggplant-Tomato Soup with Cilantro

SERVES 4 TO 6

I can't go for more than a couple of weeks without longing for eggplant. I use it in lasagna as a substitute for pasta, in soups, even in chocolate cupcakes! This soup spotlights the true flavor of eggplant. There's very little chopping here. You just cut the veggies in half, sear them in a skillet, then roast them. (I like cast-iron skillets for searing, but if you don't have cast iron, use a standard skillet.)

If you dislike eggplant because you think it's bitter-tasting, try it again. Hybrids have pretty much eliminated the bitterness in eggplant. Roasting the eggplant and tomatoes rids them of any acidity, leaving a rich, caramelized flavor. A version of this soup was a winner in one of my Iron Chef battles.

3 small eggplants (about 8 ounces each)

5 Roma tomatoes (or any peak-of-season tomatoes)

1 medium to large red onion

2 garlic cloves

4 tablespoons extra-virgin olive oil

3–4 cups homemade or store-bought chicken stock or vegetable stock (pages 231–235)

1 teaspoon kosher salt

1/2 teaspoon freshly ground black pepper
Crème fraîche, homemade (page 239) or store-bought, for garnish

2 tablespoons finely chopped fresh cilantro, for garnish

Preheat the oven to 350°F.

Cut the eggplant in half lengthwise, halve the tomatoes and the onion, and set aside. Peel the garlic cloves, place on a cutting board, and give each a good smash with your chef's knife (making sure the blade edge faces away from your palm).

Heat two large cast-iron skillets with 2 tablespoons of olive oil in each and sear all the vegetables, cut side down, until their surfaces have developed some color and are caramelized (or use one skillet and sear the vegetables in batches). Place the skillets in the oven to finish cooking. (If you're not using cast-iron skillets, be sure both pans have oven-proof handles.) When the vegetables are tender and their flesh is pierced easily with a fork, after 25 to 30 minutes, remove the skillets from the oven. Let the vegetables cool in the skillets for 10 to 20 minutes.

While the eggplant is still warm and easy to handle, scoop the flesh from the skin. Place the eggplant pulp and the other vegetables in a blender or food processor and blend with 1 cup of the stock until smooth. If you want a really velvety soup, transfer the mixture to a sieve placed over a large pot and force the mixture through to remove any remaining vegetable skins.

Place the pot over medium-high heat and slowly add 2 to 3 more cups of stock, until the soup is the desired consistency. Heat to a slow simmer. Add the salt and pepper.

Ladle into shallow soup bowls, garnish with a spoonful of crème fraîche, sprinkle with the cilantro, and serve.

# Endive, Honeydew, and Pear Salad with Honey Dressing

SERVES 4 TO 6

This spectacular salad reminds me of a still-life painting. Circle the edge of a plate with endive leaves, overlap them with juicy, fragrant slices of honeydew, top with fanned pear slices, and sprinkle with fresh mint leaves. On a hot day, this salad tastes as refreshing as it looks. Serve it with grilled chicken or just bread and cheese for a light meal.

If Bartlett pears aren't in season, go for Comice or Anjou. With honey, lighter is better for this salad, so avoid varieties with strong flavors that could overwhelm the fruit, such as chestnut honey. And if you don't spot champagne vinegar or almond oil in high-end markets or cooks' stores, see Resources (page 245).

HONEY DRESSING

1/2 cup plus 1 tablespoon almond oil or other
    light nut oil, such as walnut
3 tablespoons light-flavored honey
1/4 cup plus 1 tablespoon champagne vinegar
1/4 teaspoon kosher salt

4 large Belgian endives, washed and
    separated
1 honeydew melon
2 large Bartlett pears
8–10 large fresh mint leaves, washed and dried
1/4 cup finely chopped walnuts, for garnish
    (optional)

FOR THE HONEY DRESSING: In a small bowl, whisk together the almond oil, honey, vinegar, and salt. Refrigerate the dressing while you assemble the salad.

Place the individual endive leaves, starting with the largest ones, side by side around the edge of an oval or circular serving platter, with the narrowed end of each leaf pointing toward the platter's rim. When the outside edge is completely covered, move inward with another row of endive leaves, pointing toward the rim and overlapping the outer ring of leaves. Continue placing the leaves, saving the smallest to use in the center. Set the platter aside or place in the refrigerator if there's enough room.

Slice the honeydew in half, remove the seeds, then halve each section so that you have 4 quarters. Slice the rind off each quarter. Slice the melon crescent lengthwise into 1/2-inch-thick slices. You should have 6 to 8 crescent pieces from each quarter. Refrigerate.

Just before assembling the salad, cut the pears in half lengthwise and core them with a melon baller or a spoon. Quarter them and slice the quarters into 1/4-inch-thick slices. Set aside.

Arrange the melon slices to form a circle on top of the endive so that just the tips of

Cat's Notes  A lemon-water bath will keep your pear slices pale and creamy. Squeeze a little lemon juice—just a teaspoon or so—into a small bowl of cold water. As soon as you cut the pear slices, give them a quick dip in the lemon water.

When making the dressing, use the same spoon you used with the almond oil to measure the honey. It'll slide right off the spoon.

the endive leaves show. Make a slightly smaller circle with the pear slices, fanning them to spiral toward the center. Whisk the dressing briefly to mix and drizzle about $1/3$ cup over the salad. Pour the remainder into a serving dish to pass at the table.

Stack the mint leaves on top of one another and roll them up tightly like a cigar. Thinly slice the little roll from end to end, making long, thin strands. Finely chop the strands and sprinkle over the salad. Garnish lightly with the chopped walnuts, if you like, and serve immediately.

# Asian Steak and Spinach Salad

SERVES 4

This meal in a bowl tastes like an indulgence, with its bright green spinach, juicy strips of steak, and a soy-lime sauce that ties it all together. Hard to believe something this fast and easy to prepare is good for you too—but that's why it's one of my favorite weeknight dinners.

½ pound baby spinach
4 tablespoons extra-virgin olive oil
2 garlic cloves, minced
2 tablespoons fresh lime juice
1 teaspoon light or dark brown sugar
1 tablespoon soy sauce

1 sweet red onion, cut into ¼-inch-thick half-moons
½ pound grass-fed steak (sirloin, tenderloin, porterhouse, New York strip, or rib-eye)
1 tablespoon chopped fresh cilantro
1–2 tablespoons chopped unsalted peanuts, for garnish

Wash the spinach (see note) and spin dry or roll up the leaves in a clean dish towel. Place the spinach in a large salad bowl and set aside.

In a small bowl, mix 2 tablespoons of the olive oil, the garlic, lime juice, brown sugar, and soy sauce and set aside.

In a large cast-iron skillet, heat 1 tablespoon of the olive oil over medium-high heat. When the oil is hot but not smoking, add the onion and sauté for 2 minutes, stirring constantly. Transfer the hot onion to the salad bowl on top of the spinach. Add the remaining 1 tablespoon olive oil to the pan. Sear the steak until medium-rare, about 3 minutes per side. (If you like your steak well-done, keep it in the pan for 1 more minute.) Remove the pan from the heat, immediately transfer the steak to a cutting board, and let it rest.

Let the skillet cool for a few minutes. Add the soy-lime mixture to the pan and turn the heat to medium-high. Deglaze the pan by stirring constantly and loosening any bits of steak that cling to the bottom. Reduce the

Cat's Note  I buy prewashed spinach whenever I can. If I buy unwashed spinach—say, from a farmers' market—I fill a sink with water and put the spinach in to soak for a good 15 to 20 minutes before I start cleaning each leaf. Soaking makes the cleaning easier, but for my money, the prewashed baby spinach is worth the extra cost just to be able to skip this step.

heat to low to keep the sauce warm. Slice the meat as thin as possible, cutting against the grain. Arrange the meat slices over the onion and spinach. Drizzle with the warm sauce and sprinkle with the cilantro and peanuts. Serve immediately.

# Salmon-Topped Hash

We eat a lot of salmon (I like feeding my entire family constant hits of omega-3), so I generally cook extra fillets when I grill. Making hash with salmon during the week is easy. You can heat up a fillet that was grilled earlier or use a fresh fillet. If you have a fresh seared fillet, don't break it up but gently set it on top of the hash.

4 medium Yukon Gold potatoes, parboiled
    (page 76)
1 red bell pepper
2 tablespoons extra-virgin olive oil
1 tablespoon unsalted butter
1 medium red onion, chopped
1 teaspoon minced fresh tarragon
2 teaspoons drained capers

1 teaspoon kosher salt, plus more if desired
1/4 teaspoon freshly ground black pepper, plus
    more if desired
1 cup cubed, cooked skinned salmon
2 tablespoons crème fraîche, homemade
    (page 239) or store-bought, or sour
    cream
1 scallion, chopped, for garnish

Slip off the skins of the potatoes, grate them, and set aside.

Cut the bell pepper in half, remove the core, scrape out the seeds, and cut off any white membranes inside. Cut the pepper into neat squares.

In a large cast-iron skillet, heat the oil and butter on medium-high heat. Add the bell pepper and cook until tender and lightly browned, stirring frequently, 5 to 6 minutes. Add the onion and cook, stirring occasionally, until lightly browned, 3 to 4 minutes. Add the potatoes, tarragon, capers, salt, and pepper.

Using a spatula, press down on the mixture to crisp the potatoes and cook for about 4 minutes, then flip the hash over to cook the other side. Taste and add more salt and pepper, if you like. Slide onto a serving platter and spoon on the cubed salmon. (If using cold leftover salmon, heat it in the microwave for 20 seconds.) Top with the crème fraîche and scallion. Serve immediately.

## Cat's Note
If you're using raw salmon, preheat the oven to 200°F. Heat the olive oil and butter in the skillet over medium-high heat. Brown the salmon lightly on all sides, then transfer it to an ovenproof plate and keep it warm in the oven while you use the same skillet (you don't need to clean it) to make the rest of the hash. Place the salmon over the hash just before serving and top with the crème fraîche and scallion.

# Hash

Here is a true American comfort food. For breakfast with an egg on top, as a side dish, or for dinner with salmon on top, hash is incredibly versatile. You can make a great hash out of just about any food you like in no time. Use the recipe on page 74 as a starting point and then add the ingredients you like—chicken or turkey instead of salmon, sweet potatoes instead of Yukon Gold potatoes, plus your favorite mix of spices. (Also see the really incredible Balsamic-Glazed Duck Breast with Pear, Pearl Onion, and Mushroom Hash on page 205.)

Before you whip out your skillet, here are a few tips for hash that's crispy outside and tender inside:

◆ Use a good, heavy 10- to 12-inch skillet. I like cast iron best for this job, but you can make do with any skillet as long as it's wide enough and fairly heavy. Avoid using a new cast-iron pan for hash; a seasoned pan will turn out a better crust.

◆ Parboil the potatoes for hash, whether you're using sweet potatoes or regular potatoes, because raw ones will burn on the outside and remain hard inside. The time you spend parboiling more than makes up for the time you *don't* spend peeling. You don't need to peel potatoes when you parboil because the skins slip right off.

To parboil potatoes, fill a large pot half full of cold water. Slide in the potatoes and add more water if necessary to cover. Turn on the heat to high. When the water begins to boil, lower the heat and let simmer.

Begin checking the potatoes after 15 minutes. Pierce with a knife to test whether they're done. The knife tip should penetrate the potato but still meet some resistance, and a potato taken out of the pot should feel firm to the touch. You don't want to overcook them, because they will begin to break or crumble in the water or become waterlogged.

◆ Here's a great way to remember hash proportions: one, two, three-ones, three. That stands for 1 red bell pepper; 2 tablespoons olive oil; 1 tablespoon butter, 1 onion, 1 cup meat or fish; and 3 cups grated parboiled potatoes. Then you add salt, pepper, diced tomatoes, spices, herbs, and whatever you like. Once you've made hash a few times, play with the proportions, adding more meat, if you like, to suit your taste. For fish hashes, I use fewer potatoes so the fish isn't overwhelmed.

◆ Chop all your ingredients—the meat or fish, the bell peppers, and the onion—approximately the same size and shape. Your hash will cook more evenly and look better on the plate.

◆ The key to a great hash is control over the pan's temperature. Too hot, and the ingredients burn. Not hot enough, and the ingredients stick to the pan. Start the browning over medium-high heat, then lower the heat when you add seasonings and let the hash brown slowly. Onions and bell peppers turn black if the heat is too high.

◆ Press down on the hash with a spatula, but resist the urge to flip it more than necessary. Treat the hash more like a pancake than a stir-fry. Every 3 minutes, lift up a tiny section and peek underneath to see how the browning is coming.

◆ Warm your plates on low heat in the oven while you're cooking the hash. I think hash tastes best hot, and the warmed plates keep it that way, especially in cold weather.

# Lettuce "Gyros" Filled with Spicy Halibut

Traditional Greek gyros are made of spit-roasted lamb cut into chunks and wrapped in a warm, soft round of pita (a bread much softer and thicker than the pita we're used to), then drizzled with tzatziki.

Mine is definitely a California version, low in carbs, much lighter and—if possible—even messier than the original. Instead of lamb, I use spicy halibut fillets, and instead of bread, I serve the fish in crunchy lettuce cups. You can grill or bake the halibut. Set out a long platter with the halibut-filled lettuce cups next to a big array of condiments. Your guests can dress their gyros however they please. Be sure to pile a large stack of napkins on the table too.

HALIBUT

- 2 tablespoons extra-virgin olive oil, plus more to sear the fish and oil the baking dish
- 2 tablespoons fresh lime juice
- 1 teaspoon chili powder
- 1 tablespoon ground cumin
- 1 teaspoon cayenne pepper
- 1½ teaspoons sea salt
- ¼ teaspoon freshly ground black pepper
- 1½ pounds halibut fillets (four 6-ounce center-cut fillets or six 4-ounce fillets)

TOMATO SALAD

- 5 Roma tomatoes, diced
- 1 medium red onion, thinly sliced
- ½ cup kalamata olives, pitted and halved (see page 12)
- 1 tablespoon finely chopped fresh oregano
- 2 tablespoons coarsely chopped fresh flat-leaf parsley
- 2 tablespoons extra-virgin olive oil
- 2 tablespoons fresh lime juice
  Kosher salt and freshly ground black pepper

LETTUCE CUPS

- 1 head butter lettuce
- 1 head radicchio

CONDIMENTS

- Avocado Tzatziki (page 28) or Feta-Mint Tzatziki (page 80); optional
- Pepperoncini, drained and chopped
- Chopped scallions, for garnish

Preheat the grill to medium-hot or the oven to 350°F.

FOR THE HALIBUT: In a baking dish big enough to hold the fillets in a single layer, combine the 2 tablespoons olive oil, lime juice, chili powder, cumin, cayenne, salt, and pepper. Add the halibut fillets and turn to coat thoroughly with the marinade. Let the fillets marinate for 10 minutes to absorb the flavors while you make the tomato salad.

FOR THE TOMATO SALAD: In a medium bowl, mix the tomatoes, onion, olives, oregano, parsley, olive oil, and lime juice. Season with salt and pepper to taste and mix well. Set aside.

TO GRILL THE HALIBUT: To prevent the fish from sticking, brush the fillets with a little olive oil before placing them on the grill. Cook the fillets until they begin to turn opaque on top, 3 to 6 minutes. (For halibut steaks, grill a few minutes longer, 5 to 7 minutes.) Using a long-handled spatula, turn the fish carefully and grill on the second side for 3 to 6 minutes, until the fish is opaque throughout.

TO BAKE THE HALIBUT: Pour 1 tablespoon olive oil into a large skillet over high heat and sear the fish for 1 minute on each side. Bake the fish in an oiled Pyrex baking dish in the oven until it is firm to the touch and flakes easily when separated with the tines of a fork, 10 to 12 minutes for fillets and 12 to 15 minutes for steaks. When the fish is done, remove it from the oven and let it rest in the pan while you set out the lettuce cups on a large serving platter.

Cat's Notes   You can substitute just about any grilled fish here. Try salmon, snapper, branzino, or tuna. If you're a meat lover, try grilled pork chunks (page 27).

Premixed chili blends shorten my prep time; I keep several in my pantry. "Blackened" spice blends and spice mixes that include chili powder and orange flavor are two of my favorites, and I sprinkle them on everything from fish and meat to popcorn.

FOR THE LETTUCE CUPS: Form the lettuce cups by gently separating the heads of butter lettuce and radicchio. For extra-crisp cups, soak the lettuce leaves in very cold water for a few minutes before removing them and patting dry with paper towels. Make a cup by lining a whole leaf of butter lettuce with a radicchio leaf (you can double-line the cups if you prefer more lettuce with your gyros and want to reduce the chance of leaks).

Flake a generous portion of fish into each lettuce cup, or cut the fish into small chunks and divide evenly among the lettuce cups.

Top with the tomato salad. Drizzle with tzatziki, if using, and garnish with the pepperoncini and scallions. You can eat this with a knife and fork, or if you don't mind the drips, pick up the lettuce cup and eat it with gusto.

Serve these as soon as the hot fish hits those lettuce cups. They're great with wine, ice-cold beer, or ouzo.


## Feta-Mint Tzatziki

MAKES 1½ CUPS

Mint adds refreshing coolness and flecks of color to this twist on traditional tzatziki. Not all feta tastes the same. Try this with Greek feta or an American artisanal feta.

1 cup plain yogurt, strained through
    cheesecloth or a fine-mesh strainer
    for 30 minutes
2 tablespoons crumbled feta cheese
2 tablespoons good extra-virgin olive oil

1 tablespoon fresh lemon juice
2 teaspoons finely chopped fresh mint
1 large garlic clove, minced
1 teaspoon kosher salt
1 medium cucumber, peeled

In a medium bowl, combine all the ingredients except the cucumber. Using a box grater, grate the cucumber directly over the yogurt mixture, rotating the cucumber and grating until all the flesh is used and stopping when you reach the seeds. Stir well, then cover the bowl and refrigerate for at least an hour, or preferably overnight.

# Thai Chicken Salad with Cabbage

Cabbage is a hardworking vegetable that doesn't always get the praise it deserves. But toss it with a savory yet light dressing—made by adding store-bought Thai peanut sauce to a slightly sweet sesame oil vinaigrette—and fresh, crunchy cabbage suddenly gets the fanfare it deserves. This salad is light yet filling, and fast to make.

You can grill the chicken outdoors, poach it, or pan-sear it on top of the stove, then pop it into the oven and roast it. I think you get more flavor by grilling (the browner the bird, the more intense its flavor), but if you're not up for starting the grill, poaching is fast and easy. This salad is a good reason to throw a few extra chicken breasts on the grill when you're barbecuing over the weekend. If you have cooked chicken in the fridge, weeknight dinners are easy. You can grill boneless chicken breasts if you want, but cooking them with the bone in and the skin on adds to their flavor.

Black sesame seeds spark up the appearance of this salad, but you can use regular sesame seeds here too. You'll find black sesame seeds in the spice aisle of high-end grocery stores or Asian markets, or see Resources (page 245). Don't buy too many sesame seeds at one time; because of their high oil content, they can turn rancid. Better to buy seeds in small amounts and use them right away.

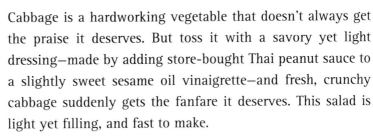

DRESSING

- ¼ cup rice wine vinegar
- ⅓ cup olive oil
- 2 teaspoons sesame oil
- 2 tablespoons store-bought Thai peanut sauce
- 2 tablespoons sugar
- 1 tablespoon black sesame seeds (see headnote)

- 1 whole chicken breast or 2 half breasts
- 1 tablespoon extra-virgin olive oil if pan-searing
- ½ head napa cabbage
- 3 large carrots
- 6 scallions
- Freshly ground black pepper

FOR THE DRESSING: In a medium bowl, whisk together all the ingredients. Set aside.

TO GRILL THE CHICKEN: Preheat the grill. When the coals are medium-hot, place the chicken breasts on the grill so that they're not directly over the flame. Cook the chicken for 6 to 8 minutes per side, turning only once to keep the grill marks clear and distinct. Remove from the grill and set aside to cool.

TO POACH THE CHICKEN: Skin the chicken breasts and gently slide them into a pot of simmering water. Cook for about 20 minutes, then remove the chicken with tongs or a slotted spoon and drain in a colander.

TO PAN-SEAR AND ROAST THE CHICKEN: Preheat the oven to 375°F. Pour the olive oil into an ovenproof skillet set over medium-high heat. Place the chicken breasts in the skillet skin side down, sear for just 1 minute, then turn them over and cook for 1 more minute. Slide the pan into the hot oven and roast the chicken for 5 minutes. Lower the oven temperature to 350°F and cook for another 15 to 20 minutes. Remove from the oven and set aside to cool.

Meanwhile, thinly slice the cabbage (you should have about 8 cups). Grate the carrots (about 1 cup), using a box grater or a food processor with the shredder disk. If you're not assembling the salad immediately, cover the vegetables and place in the refrigerator. Thinly slice the scallions, setting aside about 2 sliced scallions for a garnish.

Shred the chicken, discarding the skin and bones. In a large salad bowl, toss together the cabbage, carrots, chicken, and scallions. Pour the dressing over the salad and toss. Sprinkle with pepper and the remaining scallions. Serve.

# Curried Red Snapper

This is an exciting way to prepare red snapper. The fish stands up to the spices, and this dish cooks in about 20 minutes, so it's great on a weeknight.

For a simple meal, serve with basmati rice and a green salad. For a tropical party, set out this curry with Grilled Watermelon and Shrimp (page 152) and Shrimp and Scallop Coconut Seviche (page 60). Serve with Mango Margaritas (page 184) or Classic Mojitos (page 116).

2 pounds red snapper fillets

2 scallions, chopped

3 tablespoons curry powder

2 teaspoons kosher salt

1 teaspoon freshly ground black pepper

1/4 cup extra-virgin olive oil

2 tablespoons unsalted butter

1–2 Scotch bonnet peppers, halved and seeded (see note)

1 garlic clove, crushed

2 cups unsweetened coconut milk

1 cup water

2 large tomatoes, coarsely chopped, or 1 cup coarsely chopped canned, peeled tomatoes

2 medium onions, cut into 1/4-inch-thick slices

3–4 sprigs fresh cilantro

**Cat's Note**   Curry powder, cilantro, and peppers provide a lot of spice here, but the coconut milk smooths the flavors and balances the heat. Scotch bonnet peppers are extremely hot. You may want to start with one Scotch bonnet pepper for a milder dish.

Cut the red snapper into 3/4- to 1-inch pieces and place in a large bowl. Add the scallions, curry powder, salt, and pepper. Stir gently, cover, and refrigerate for at least an hour.

When you are ready to cook, heat the olive oil and butter over medium-high heat in a 10- to 12-inch skillet. Add the fish and cook, stirring, until the pieces are lightly browned. Add the peppers, garlic, coconut milk, water, tomatoes, and onions, cover, and bring to a boil. Reduce the heat to low and simmer until the fish is tender, 20 to 25 minutes. Sprinkle the cilantro leaves on top of the dish as a garnish. Serve.

# Grilled Skirt Steak with Shiitake Mushroom Salsa

SERVES 4

Skirt steak is relatively inexpensive, but it's really tasty and cooks in no time. The beef gets a boost from a marinade of lime juice, honey, soy, and fresh ginger. An hour or two is enough; overnight is even better.

Serve with warm tortillas, if you like, or a mound of cool, crisp greens. This salsa is a great topping for bruschetta.

MARINADE

- 4–5 garlic cloves, chopped
- 1 1/2 tablespoons peeled, grated fresh ginger
- 2 tablespoons plus 1 teaspoon lime juice (from 2 large limes)
- 1/4 cup soy sauce
- 1/4 cup plus 2 tablespoons extra-virgin olive oil
- 1 1/2 tablespoons honey
- 2 tablespoons kosher salt
- 1/4 teaspoon freshly ground black pepper

- 2 pounds skirt steak

SHIITAKE MUSHROOM SALSA

- 3 tablespoons extra-virgin olive oil
- 2 1/2 cups sliced shiitake mushrooms (about 1/2 pound)
- 2 large shallots, sliced into rings
- 1 small red chili, sliced into rings
- 1 tablespoon chopped fresh cilantro
- 2 tablespoons sesame oil
- 1 tablespoon rice wine vinegar
- 2 tablespoons chopped scallions
- 1 teaspoon kosher salt
- 1/2 teaspoon freshly ground black pepper

FOR THE MARINADE: In a large bowl, mix together the garlic, ginger, lime juice, soy sauce, olive oil, honey, salt, and pepper to make a paste. Rub this mixture over the steak, place the steak in a shallow dish, cover, and marinate for at least 1 hour, or preferably overnight in the refrigerator. Bring to room temperature before grilling.

Preheat the grill.

Just before you put the steak on the grill, prepare the shiitake salsa.

## Cat's Note

To peel the ginger easily, scrape off the skin with a spoon.

FOR THE SHIITAKE MUSHROOM SALSA: Pour the olive oil into a large skillet and turn the heat to high. When the oil is hot, add the mushrooms. Lower the heat to medium-high. Sauté until golden brown, about 4 minutes. Add the shallots and chili and sauté until the shallots just begin to turn golden, 2 to 3 minutes. Remove the pan from the heat and transfer the mushroom mixture to a bowl to cool. Add the cilantro, sesame oil, vinegar, scallions, salt, and pepper and toss lightly.

Remove the skirt steak from the marinade and place on the grill over medium-hot coals. Cook until the steak is crusted on all sides but still medium-rare inside, 3 to 4 minutes per side. Remove the steak from the grill and let it rest for 5 to 10 minutes. Cut into 1-inch-thick slices and serve with a spoonful of salsa on top.

# Pasta with Roasted Pepper and Tomato Sauce

SERVES 4 TO 6

Luscious, with terrific sun-drenched flavor and a brilliant color, this sauce is easy to whirl up in your blender or food processor if you simply roast a few extra tomatoes and peppers whenever you make Romesco Sauce (page 146). Then pop the sauce into the freezer and pull it out any day you need a satisfying meal in a hurry.

When whirling hot liquid in your blender, be extra cautious: use a thick dish towel and keep your hand on the lid to prevent it from flying off.

Kosher salt

1 tablespoon extra-virgin olive oil

2–3 garlic cloves, minced

2 red bell peppers, roasted (page 242), peeled, seeded, and coarsely chopped

1 pint (about 30) cherry tomatoes, roasted (page 241)

1½ cups chicken stock, homemade (pages 231–233) or store-bought

1 pound dried fettuccine, spaghetti, or capellini

½ cup heavy cream (optional)

⅛ teaspoon freshly ground black pepper

Freshly grated Parmesan cheese, for garnish

Leaves from 4 sprigs of fresh flat-leaf parsley, chopped, for garnish

Cat's Note   Although the heavy cream is optional, I find that a little bit smooths away the last bit of acidity from the tomatoes and peppers and results in a much richer sauce.

Fill a large pot or a pasta pot fitted with a strainer with water, add 1 tablespoon salt, and bring to a boil.

Meanwhile, heat the olive oil in a large skillet. Add the garlic and cook for 1 to 2 minutes, or until it softens. Add the peppers and tomatoes and cook for 1 minute. Stir in the chicken stock. Bring to a simmer and let cook for 2 to 3 minutes. Remove the skillet from the stove and let the mixture cool for 5 to 10 minutes. Whirl the tomato mixture in a food processor or a blender, taking care to cover the lid with a towel and hold it on tightly if using a blender. Process or blend until smooth. Set aside.

When the water in the pot is boiling, add the pasta and cook, stirring occasionally, until al dente.

While the pasta is cooking, pour the tomato mixture back into the skillet and set over low heat. Add the cream, if using, and heat gently, adding $1/2$ teaspoon salt and the pepper. Taste and adjust the seasonings.

Drain the pasta and transfer to a large serving bowl. Ladle on the tomato sauce and garnish with a little Parmesan and parsley. Serve immediately.

# Farfalle and Herb Salad with Peas

A pasta salad is a good dish to have in your repertoire, and this one, with its butterfly-shaped pasta, shines. Just be sure to choose fresh, bright herbs. For pasta salads, cook the pasta a little less than you would for a hot pasta dish.

3 teaspoons kosher salt

1 pound farfalle or orzo

3/4 cup peas (blanched if fresh)

1/4 cup finely chopped fresh flat-leaf parsley

2 tablespoons chopped fresh chives

1 teaspoon chopped fresh oregano

1 teaspoon chopped fresh mint

3 garlic cloves, minced

5 tablespoons fresh lemon juice (from 2 large lemons)

1 1/2 cups halved cherry tomatoes

2 tablespoons extra-virgin olive oil

Bring a large pot of water to a boil over high heat. Add 2 teaspoons of the salt to the boiling water, then add the farfalle. Cook for 7 minutes, or until the pasta is done but still firm. Drain the pasta in a colander, rinse with cold water, and drain again.

In a large serving bowl, combine the pasta, peas, herbs, garlic, lemon juice, and the remaining 1 teaspoon salt. Toss and mix well. Add the cherry tomatoes, drizzle with the olive oil, and toss gently. Serve or cover and refrigerate until you're ready to serve. (The salad can be prepared a day ahead, covered, and refrigerated.)

# White Cheddar Corn Bread with Scallions

This is a no-fail recipe that you can whip up in your food processor in no time at all. (You can also use an electric mixer.) The raw sugar adds a richer flavor, but you can use regular sugar with no problem.

| | |
|---|---|
| 8 tablespoons (1 stick) unsalted butter, softened, plus more for the baking dish | 1 large egg, lightly beaten |
| | ½ teaspoon raw sugar (see headnote) |
| | ½ teaspoon salt |
| 1 cup cornmeal | 1 scallion, chopped |
| 1 cup all-purpose flour | ½ cup grated white cheddar cheese |
| 1 tablespoon baking powder | 1⅓ cups whole milk |

Place a rack in the middle of the oven and preheat the oven to 400°F. Butter an 8-inch square baking dish and set aside.

In a food processor, combine the butter, cornmeal, flour, baking powder, egg, sugar, and salt. Process for 20 to 30 seconds, until blended. Add the scallion and the cheese and pulse for a few seconds just to combine. Pour the milk through the feed tube and process until blended well. Lift the lid of the processor and scrape the sides and bottom with a spatula to check for lumps. If you find any, replace the lid and pulse for another few seconds. You can also use an electric mixer to combine all the ingredients.

Pour the batter into the prepared baking dish and bake for about 25 minutes. Watch the corn bread closely, and don't wait until it's brown on top to remove it from the oven. Cut into squares and serve immediately.

OPTION: Corn Bread Madeleines

These savory madeleines aren't hard to make, but they look very special.

Lightly butter a madeleine pan and sprinkle the greased molds lightly with flour. Turn the pan upside down and tap it lightly to shake off excess flour. (If you have a Teflon madeleine pan, you can skip this step.) Set the pan aside.

Spoon about 1½ tablespoons of batter into each mold, until the batter is level with the top of the pan. Smooth the tops with an offset spatula or a knife and wipe away any excess batter. Bake for 12 to 15 minutes, or until the edges are golden brown and the tops are firm when lightly touched. These are best served warm from the oven.

# Curried Lentils with Butternut Squash

For such a homey dish, this has a lot of pizzazz, thanks to the fresh ginger, curry, and chili powder. It's a healthy alternative to chili, and I make it for the football crowds every autumn. Served with fresh mango chutney, brown rice, and a frosty mug of cold beer, this good-for-you meal seems like comfort food.

If you have a microwave, you can cook the squash cubes in a microwave-safe casserole dish until tender—about 6 minutes on high. You don't need to add any water to the dish.

1 cup lentils (preferably French, or green, lentils; available in specialty stores and health-food stores)

1 small butternut squash (about 1½ pounds), peeled and cut into chunks

1 tablespoon extra-virgin olive oil

1 tablespoon curry powder

1 teaspoon grated fresh ginger

1 teaspoon chili powder

Kosher salt and freshly ground black pepper

¼ cup unsweetened shredded coconut (optional)

## Cat's Note
Take care when peeling the squash, as squash skin is tough and slippery. I use a serrated knife and cut slowly. I also use a clean dish towel to hold the squash and keep it from sliding.

Butter an 8-by-11-inch baking dish and set aside.

Pour the lentils into a large saucepan and cover with cold water. Bring to a boil, reduce the heat to medium-low, and add the squash. Simmer until the squash is soft, the lentils are tender, and the liquid is reduced by two thirds, about 25 minutes. Remove from the heat and drain. Use tongs or a slotted spoon to transfer the chunks of squash to a medium bowl, then mash them roughly with a fork or a potato masher or put them through a ricer.

Preheat the oven to 375°F.

In a large bowl, mix the lentils and the squash with the olive oil, curry powder, ginger, chili powder, and salt and pepper to taste. Spoon the mixture into the prepared baking dish. (At this point, you can cover the dish and refrigerate it for a few hours or overnight.) Bake until piping hot, about 20 minutes if you put it into the oven right after mixing and 25 to 30 minutes if it's been refrigerated.

Serve warm, garnished with shredded coconut, if you like.

Easy

# Roasted Sweet Potatoes with Rosemary and Orange

1 large unpeeled sweet potato per person
Extra-virgin olive oil
Fresh rosemary
Sea salt
Freshly ground black pepper
1 orange for every 2 potatoes

Preheat the oven to 350°F. Wash the sweet potatoes well and dry with a clean dish towel. Slice each potato in half lengthwise.

Oil a glass baking dish or a standard baking sheet with sides. Pour 1 tablespoon olive oil into a small bowl. Pour less oil into the bowl than you think you'll need and add more if you run low. Dip your fingers into the olive oil and rub oil over each sweet potato half, both the cut surface and the skin. When each potato half is coated, place it in the dish or on the baking sheet, cut side up.

On gray, chilly evenings, I come home from work, pop these into the oven, pull on my sweats, and unwind with my son. By the time we're all ready to eat, these potatoes are done—and just the thing to warm us up.

It's easy to cook from the hip with this one. Substitute parsley for the rosemary and finish with lime juice and a sprinkle of Citrus-Flavored Salt (page 244) instead of orange juice and sea salt. I like to roast one or two extra sweet potatoes when I prepare this dish and use them to make hash later in the week.

Coarsely chop the rosemary and sprinkle it over the potatoes. Sprinkle with salt and pepper to taste. Slide the pan into the oven and roast the potatoes for 40 to 50 minutes.

When the potatoes are just about ready, roll the oranges between your palm and the countertop to get the juices flowing, then juice the oranges and set the juice aside. (If you like, you can zest the oranges before squeezing them and toss a tiny bit of zest into the juice.)

As soon as the potatoes come out of the oven, score the cut surface of each potato using a sharp knife, making a slight checkerboard pattern. (Protect your fingers by holding the potato with a clean dish towel.) Spoon a little juice over the top of each potato. Don't drown them; just give them a bright hit of citrus to balance the rosemary, salt, and pepper. Cool the potatoes for 10 minutes before serving.

# Rizogalo (Creamy Rice Pudding)

*Rizo* means rice in Greek, and *galo* means milk. The creamy rice pudding *rizogalo* is a standard in every Greek taverna. This version is a little different because you make it with leftover rice.

You wouldn't expect leftover rice to be transformed into a rice pudding this smooth and fragrant. The aroma comes from adding the zest of a whole lemon plus scraping the inside of a vanilla bean. It might seem odd to rinse cooked rice, but don't skip this step, or the pudding will be thick and starchy instead of light and fluffy.

| | |
|---|---|
| 6 whole almonds, toasted (see note on page 7) | 1/2 cup sugar |
| 2 cups cooked rice (warm or cold) | 1/8 teaspoon salt |
| 2 1/2 cups whole milk | Finely grated zest of 1 lemon |
| 1 whole vanilla bean or 2 teaspoons vanilla extract | 1 large egg, lightly beaten |
| | 1 1/2 teaspoons unsalted butter |
| | 1 teaspoon ground cinnamon |

Place a toasted almond in each of the ramekins or pudding bowls and set aside.

Place the rice in a large bowl and rinse with cool water. Pour the rice into a strainer and drain well. Set aside.

Pour the milk into a large saucepan. Split the surface of the vanilla bean lengthwise down the center with the tip of a paring knife. Push the side of the knife down the center of the bean to open it up, loosening the tiny seeds of the pod. Put the whole pod with the seeds into the milk. (If using vanilla extract, don't add it yet.)

Place the saucepan over medium-high heat and bring to a low boil. Reduce the heat to low and whisk in the sugar, salt, and lemon zest. Ladle about 1/4 cup of the hot milk mixture very slowly into the beaten egg while whisking gently. (This technique tempers the liquid so that the egg won't scramble.) Pour the egg mixture into the saucepan, stirring to combine with the remaining hot milk. Add the rice and raise the heat to medium-high. Stir constantly over low heat until the mixture begins to thicken, about 10 minutes. Stir in the butter and vanilla extract, if using. Immediately spoon the pudding into the ramekins or bowls. Sprinkle lightly with the cinnamon. Serve warm or chilled.

# Cherry Clafouti

A clafouti combines the creaminess of a pudding and the texture of a cake but is easier to make than either one. Cherries are great in a clafouti, and I'm going to suggest something controversial: try making this with whole, unpitted cherries. Leaving the pits in means the cherries hold their shape and juice during cooking, and spitting out the pits is no big deal—it's the same as eating whole olives. Of course, if you have children at your table, you'll want to pit the cherries first, but for grown-ups, try it both ways, with pitted and unpitted cherries, and see which you prefer. (If you do leave in pits, alert your guests!)

You can also make a much faster—and still very delicious—clafouti in a blender (see the options at the end of the recipe). You can use almost any fruit, as long as it's fresh and at the peak of its season. In summer, substitute or add plums or sliced peaches or nectarines, or try a combination of fruit.

Serve this warm from the oven with ice cream or softly whipped cream.

Easy

2½ tablespoons unsalted butter, plus more to butter the baking dish

1½ pounds fresh cherries, stemmed and washed, pitted or unpitted

4–6 tablespoons sugar, depending on sweetness of cherries, plus ¼ cup

Finely grated zest of 1 lemon

4 large eggs, at room temperature, separated

⅓ cup whole milk

⅓ cup heavy cream

6 tablespoons all-purpose flour

2 teaspoons vanilla extract

⅛ teaspoon salt

¼ cup confectioners' sugar

Place a rack in the middle of the oven and preheat the oven to 375°F. Lightly butter the sides and bottom of a 2-quart baking dish or 10- to 11-inch pie plate.

In a large skillet over medium heat, melt the butter. Add the cherries and sprinkle with the 4 to 6 tablespoons sugar. Add the lemon zest. Stir gently for 5 to 7 minutes, until the cherries are heated through and slightly tender and the sugar has dissolved and combined with the juices. Remove from the heat and distribute evenly in the bottom of the prepared baking dish. Set aside.

Place the egg yolks and the remaining ¼ cup sugar in a large bowl. With a hand mixer, beat on medium-high until the mixture is light yellow, fluffy, and thickened. Stop the mixer and add the milk, cream, and flour. Blend on low speed until the mixture is well combined. With a rubber spatula, scrape the sides and bottom of the bowl. Add the vanilla and mix briefly to incorporate well.

Clean the beaters. Then, in a separate large bowl, beat the egg whites and salt with the hand mixer until the whites hold soft peaks. Gently fold about one third of the whites into the yolk mixture with a rubber spatula. Fold in the remaining whites until they are well incorporated. Pour the batter over the cherries in the baking dish.

Bake for about 20 minutes, until the clafouti is puffed. Open the oven and sprinkle the top with the confectioners' sugar. Bake for another 10 minutes, or until the clafouti has puffed slightly more and is firm to the touch. Remove from the oven and place on a rack to cool. Serve slightly warm or cool.

## OPTION 1: Blueberry Ginger Blender Clafouti

3 cups blueberries, rinsed

2 tablespoons chopped candied ginger

1/4 cup plus 1 tablespoon sugar

1 cup whole milk

3 large eggs

1/2 cup all-purpose flour

2 teaspoons vanilla extract

Preheat the oven to 325°F. Lightly butter the sides and bottom of a 2-quart baking dish or 10- to 11-inch pie plate.

Arrange the blueberries and the ginger in the bottom of the prepared baking dish and sprinkle with the 1/4 cup sugar.

Pour the milk into the blender and add the eggs, flour, vanilla, and the remaining 1 tablespoon sugar. Blend on high speed until mixed, about 30 seconds.

Pour the batter over the fruit in the baking dish. Bake for 25 to 30 minutes, or until the clafouti is lightly browned on the edges. Serve while still warm.

## OPTION 2: Cherry Ginger Blender Clafouti

Follow the Blueberry Ginger recipe, substituting 3 cups pitted fresh cherries for the blueberries.

## OPTION 3: Peach Ginger Blender Clafouti

Follow the Blueberry Ginger recipe, substituting 3 cups fresh peach chunks for the blueberries. You can peel the peaches or not.

## OPTION 4: Summer Fruit Combo Blender Clafouti

Follow the Blueberry Ginger recipe, substituting 3 cups of a combination of ripe, fresh summer fruits for the blueberries: try berries, peaches, and cherries.

# Pantry Makeover
# Salt, Sugar, Flour, and Cornmeal

You probably already have these four staples in your pantry, but a few variations on the standards will give you some flexibility. Here's what I keep in my pantry at home.

## Salt

The two salts I always have on hand are kosher salt and gray salt. I'm never without them. I used kosher salt for the basics—tossing into pasta water or for salt-roasting a pan of baby beets. Gray salt is the purest sea salt, and I use this as a condiment for a final sprinkling on a salad or a really good steak. Gray salt is moist and chunky. You can use it as is or dry it, but don't store it in a standard salt grinder with metal blades, because it will rust the metal. Many stores carry gray salt, but if you have trouble finding it, go to Napastyle.com, where you'll also find salt grinders with ceramic blades, which are made to hold gray salt.

## Sugar

You'll need granulated sugar, confectioners' sugar, dark brown sugar, and light brown sugar. I also like raw sugar and coarse-textured demerara sugar, a raw sugar that looks like slightly moist crystals, just right for sprinkling over breads and cookies before baking.

## Flour

I keep this pretty simple and stock all-purpose flour, cake flour, and Wondra flour, which is a little smoother, for use in gravies. I also have rice flour on hand, because it's nice and light for frying, and I like buckwheat flour for pancakes.

## Cornmeal

You'll find three kinds of cornmeal in my pantry: standard, polenta-grade, and semolina. I use standard cornmeal for frying trout or tossing onto the pan before cooking a pizza. I use the polenta-grade cornmeal, which is slightly finer, to make polenta, and I use semolina cornmeal to make pizza crust.

Too often guests stand around sipping wine and wishing they could help while the cook feverishly works alone. Not with these recipes. They're made so that your friends and family can pitch in and have a blast.

## Appetizers

Eggplant Dip    105

Bruschetta with Three Toppings    106

Dolmathes (Grape Leaves Stuffed
    with Rice and Herbs)    112

## Drinks

Classic Mojitos    116

Sake Margaritas    117

White Peach Sangria    118

## Salads

Fuji Apple, Walnut, and Dill Salad    119

Baby Greens and Figs Stuffed
    with Gorgonzola Cheese    121

## Main Dishes

Sunday Cheesesteak Sandwiches
    with Homemade Provolone Sauce    122

Saffron Potato Omelet    125

Crispy "Fried" Chicken    128

The Zoran Roll    131

Tropical Fruit and Jerk Chicken Sushi    135

Prosciutto, Pear, and Blue Cheese Sushi    137

Chicken Potpie with Puff Pastry    140

Salmon and Scallop Skewers with Romesco Sauce    145

Vegetable Couscous en Crépinettes    148

Goat Cheese Fondue    151

Grilled Watermelon and Shrimp    152

Basic Crepes    157

Wild Mushroom and Kasseri Crepes    158

## Side Dishes

To-Die-For Garlic Mashed Potatoes    159

Creamed Pearl Onions and Peanuts    160

COOKING WITHOUT MEASURING: Grilled Vegetables
    with Orange Mayo    162

## Desserts

Lemonade Cookies    164

Lemon, Butter, and Sugar Crepes    166

Chocolate Budino    171

Banana Chocolate-Chunk Ice Cream    172

# Eggplant Dip

I love this way of cooking eggplant: poke it all over with a fork, roast it for 45 minutes, then whirl it in a food processor. This satiny dip highlights the eggplant's flavor with garlic and lemon juice. If you want to spice it up, add the Moroccan spices in the option below. Serve with baguette slices or pita wedges. For a great party food, spoon this dip into endive spears and arrange the endive on a platter.

2 large eggplants (about 1 pound each)
5 garlic cloves, coarsely chopped
3 tablespoons fresh lemon juice
1 teaspoon kosher salt
¼ teaspoon freshly ground black pepper

½ cup extra-virgin olive oil
2 tablespoons coarsely chopped walnuts (optional)
1 tablespoon chopped fresh flat-leaf parsley (optional)

Preheat the oven to 400°F.

Place the whole eggplants on a baking sheet and pierce each one with a fork in several places. Bake them for 45 minutes, or until the eggplants have collapsed and the pulp is completely soft. Remove from the oven and let cool for 10 to 20 minutes. While the eggplants are still warm, split each one in half and scoop out the pulp with a large spoon. Discard the stems and skin.

Toss the garlic into the food processor and pulse a few times. Add the eggplant, lemon juice, salt, and pepper and process until smooth. Slowly pour the olive oil through the feed tube while processing. Scrape the dip into a serving bowl. If you like, stir in the walnuts and sprinkle with the parsley. Cover and refrigerate until ready to serve.

OPTION: Moroccan Eggplant Dip

Before pouring the olive oil into the food processor, add 1 teaspoon ground cumin, ½ teaspoon ground coriander, and ⅛ teaspoon cayenne pepper to the eggplant mixture. Garnish with chopped fresh cilantro, if you like, instead of parsley.

# Bruschetta with Three Toppings

Bruschetta brings out the soul of two simple ingredients: bread and tomatoes. The bread has to be thick slices of a good rustic bread, and the tomatoes have to be those of summer—the ones you think about so longingly in mid-January.

Once you have the bread and tomatoes, all you need is a little salt, olive oil, and garlic, and you have the basic bruschetta. Start by toasting the bread, preferably over a fire, since *bruschetta* comes from the Italian word *bruscare*, "to roast over coals." From there you can go in a hundred different directions. You can make the classic bruschetta, with chunks of heirloom tomatoes and finely cut fresh basil, or try a topping of feta and kalamata olives or sweet red peppers and shavings of Asiago cheese.

If you want to make a party of it, stock up on baguettes, make all three toppings, and set out a few bottles of chilled Pinot Grigio. Encourage your guests to eat their bruschetta with their fingers. When you sit down, enjoy the bruschetta, as the Italians say, *piano, piano,* "slowly, slowly."

1 baguette, cut into ½-inch-thick slices

2 tablespoons extra-virgin olive oil

1 garlic clove, cut in half

Toppings (recipes follow)

To give the bread slices maximum flavor, toast them on the grill. Lightly brush both sides of each slice with olive oil and grill for just a minute on each side. Use tongs to turn them and make sure the bread doesn't get too dark. (You can also toast them in your oven. Preheat the oven to 425°F and brush the slices with olive oil. Arrange the slices on an ungreased baking sheet and bake for 10 minutes, turning once, until crisp and light brown.)

When the slices are just the right shade of golden brown to suit your taste, hold each warm slice (protecting your fingers with a clean dish towel) and rub the cut side of the garlic clove completely over the bread, front and back. The heat and crispiness will "melt" the garlic, flavoring the bread perfectly. Top with any of the three toppings suggested here, or come up with your own.

OK, I admit it. When I'm grilling, I don't relinquish the tongs easily. But your guests can toast their own bread on the grill while you bring out more wine or cut more slices of bread.

## Tomato and Basil

MAKES ABOUT ¾ CUP, TOPS 12 TO 16 BRUSCHETTA

Make sure the tomatoes are fantastic, and use your very best olive oil and salt here.

6–8 large ripe tomatoes (½ tomato for each
    slice of bread)
12–16 fresh basil leaves

Sea salt
Extra-virgin olive oil

Cut the tomatoes into small chunks about the size of the tip of your little finger. Cut the basil leaves into a chiffonade by stacking 4 or 5 leaves, rolling them like a cigar, and then, starting at the tip and working toward the stem, cutting thin strips. This will give you small, fine ribbons of basil.

Spoon a good helping of tomatoes onto the bruschetta. (Don't be stingy; I like the tomatoes to be piled up and overflowing the bread slice.) Sprinkle generously with basil chiffonade. Add a light pinch of salt and drizzle with olive oil. Serve immediately.

## Kalamata Olive and Feta Cheese

MAKES ABOUT ½ CUP, TOPS 18 BRUSCHETTA

Think of this tangy mix of olives, feta, lemon, and red pepper flakes as a base and add whatever you like: chunks of fresh tomato or roasted cherry tomatoes, a few tiny cucumber cubes, or sautéed mushrooms.

2 tablespoons crumbled feta cheese
1 tablespoon fresh lemon juice
1 teaspoon crushed red pepper flakes

¼ cup coarsely chopped kalamata olives
1 teaspoon coarsely chopped fresh oregano
½ teaspoon top-quality extra-virgin olive oil

Combine all the ingredients in a small bowl. With this topping, I like to spread a thin coating on my bruschetta, but add as much as you like. Spoon onto warm bruschetta and serve.

## Sweet Red Peppers with Asiago Cheese

MAKES ¾ CUP, TOPS 24 BRUSCHETTA

I always keep jars of sweet red pepper strips in my pantry, but just as often I roast my own peppers, especially when they're in season. If you want to roast your own, follow the tips on page 242. I like just a little Asiago on my bruschetta, but if you want a cheesier version, go ahead and add more.

1 7-ounce jar roasted sweet red pepper
    strips, drained and coarsely chopped
2 teaspoons drained capers
3 tablespoons chopped fresh basil
1 tablespoon balsamic vinegar

2 teaspoons fresh lemon juice
1 teaspoon kosher salt
½ teaspoon freshly ground black pepper
2 tablespoons shaved Asiago cheese, plus
    more if desired

In a small bowl, combine all the ingredients except the cheese. Spread on the bruschetta. Sprinkle each bruschetta with a few shavings of cheese.

Cat's Note   To shave hard cheeses such as Asiago and Parmesan, use a vegetable peeler or a cheese slicer.

# Dolmathes
# for Non-Greeks

If you've never made dolmathes before, here are some tips to get you rolling.

Look for grape leaves in clear glass jars. The leaves should be dark green; avoid jars with yellowish leaves.

Sometimes the grape leaves are packed very tightly. Don't try to pull them out one by one, because they'll tear. Instead, push your fingers into the jar, grab the whole bundle, and twist as you pull it out.

Open up the bundle with your fingers and gently pull the leaves free one at a time. Position the first leaf so the shiny side faces down and the stem is pointing toward you. Some leaves may have small holes or tears. Don't worry if the holes are small; choose a different leaf if the holes are big.

I use a generous teaspoon of rice, but sometimes the grape leaves will be bigger and sometimes smaller, so you'll want to use more filling or less. Place the filling in the center of the leaf above the stem.

Start by rolling the bottom edge (stem end) over the rice. Now bring in one of the pointy sections of the leaf from the left or right. You can bring the left section of the leaf in at an angle so it wraps more neatly and tightly around your rice bundle. Wrap the grape leaf as securely as you can around the rice so it doesn't unroll during cooking.

The more bundles you make, the easier it is to get the hang of it. The next time it will be a snap.

# Dolmathes (Grape Leaves Stuffed with Rice and Herbs)

These savory little bundles are rolled in grape leaves and served with a velvety egg-lemon sauce. There are two tricks to making dolmathes, and neither is hard to master. The first is rolling the grape leaves around the rice filling. Just follow the steps on page 110. (And remember, the more people you have rolling, the faster this dish goes into the oven.)

The second trick is tempering the egg and lemon mixture with a few spoonfuls of the hot stock. This is easy too. Adding just a little hot liquid while whisking prevents the eggs from curdling.

$^2/_3$ cup cooked long-grain white rice

2 cups minced onions (about 2 medium onions)

1 teaspoon finely chopped fresh mint

2 teaspoons finely chopped fresh oregano

2 teaspoons finely chopped fresh parsley

$^3/_4$ teaspoon kosher salt

$^1/_4$ teaspoon freshly ground black pepper

1 7-ounce jar brined grape leaves (36 leaves)

1 cup chicken stock or water, plus more if needed

3 large eggs

$^1/_2$ cup plus 1 tablespoon fresh lemon juice (from 4 large lemons)

## Cat's Note

Yes, chefs order Chinese takeout too. I always order extra rice so I can make dolmathes. (Leftover rice never had it so good.) Or sometimes I make it into a sweet, creamy rice pudding called Rizogalo (page 95).

Preheat the oven to 350°F.

In a large bowl, combine the rice, onions, herbs, salt, and pepper. Cover and refrigerate until ready to use.

When you're ready to roll up the dolmathes, carefully pull the grape leaves from the jar and separate them. Place each leaf on a cutting board, shiny side down, with its stem toward you. Put a generous teaspoon of the rice mixture on top of the leaf near the bottom, fold the bottom over the filling, then fold in each of the sides to cover the filling completely. Roll tightly toward the tip of the leaf, as if you're rolling up a towel.

Place the rolled grape leaves in a 9-by-13-inch baking dish, seam side down, and lay a few of the remaining grape leaves on top of the dolmathes to keep them from unrolling. Pour the stock over the dolmathes, covering the rolls completely. Bake for 45 minutes, or until the grape leaves are tender. Check after 30 minutes and add more stock, if necessary, to keep the dolmathes covered.

Shortly before the dolmathes are finished baking, whisk the eggs and lemon juice together in a small bowl. Set aside. Check to see whether the dolmathes are hot throughout by eating one. When the dolmathes are ready—they'll be crinkly and fork-tender—remove the dish from the oven. With tongs, remove and discard the top flat grape leaves, then gently lift out each dolma and transfer it to a plate. Loosely cover the plate with foil and set it aside while you make the sauce.

Carefully drain the hot stock from the casserole dish into a medium bowl. Slowly dribble the hot stock into the egg and lemon mixture, starting with just 1 or 2 tablespoons and whisking constantly to prevent the eggs from curdling. With tongs, transfer the dolmathes back to the casserole dish and pour the stock mixture over them. Allow the dolmathes to rest for 10 minutes while the sauce thickens. The dolmathes are good warm or cold.

# Classic Mojitos·

The fragrance of fresh mint and lime always lifts my spirits. This is good with rum—no, it's *great* with rum—but I sometimes make it without the alcohol, simply adding more club soda or a little ginger ale. I rim the glasses with superfine sugar, but use regular sugar if that's what you have in your cupboard. Most mojitos come stuffed with mint leaves. You can either muddle the leaves in a cocktail shaker and strain the drink into glasses or add fine ribbons of mint to each drink just before serving.

4 tablespoons sugar, plus 2 tablespoons (preferably superfine) to coat the rims of the glasses

6–8 medium to large very juicy limes

12–14 mint sprigs, rinsed in cool water

¾ cup (6 ounces) light rum

4 cups ice cubes

½ cup club soda

Place a sheet of foil in your freezer so that you have a spot to chill your sugar-rimmed glasses. Pour the 2 tablespoons sugar onto a small, flat saucer. Halve 1 of the limes crosswise. Cut one half into slices and set aside for the garnish. Holding a glass upside down so that the lime juice doesn't run down the outside, rub the cut surface of the remaining lime half around the glass's rim. Immediately dip the glass into the saucer of sugar to coat the rim all the way around. Gently shake off any excess sugar and carefully place the glass upright on the sheet of foil in the freezer. Repeat with the other 3 glasses, using the same lime half.

Juice the remaining limes and set aside. You should have 6 to 8 tablespoons lime juice.

If you'd like to add fine mint ribbons to your drinks, stack 4 to 6 mint leaves per serving, roll the leaves up like a cigar, and cut across the roll, slicing the mint into fine strips. Set these aside and, using your hands, tear apart 5 or 6 mint sprigs and toss them into a cocktail shaker. Pour in the lime juice, rum, and the remaining 4 tablespoons sugar. Using a wooden spoon, muddle this together, crushing the mint leaves to release all that fragrant mint oil. Cap the shaker and shake well.

Remove the sugar-rimmed glasses from the freezer and toss a handful of ice into each glass. Strain the drinks from the cocktail shaker into the glasses. Divide the mint ribbons, if you like, among the four glasses, and top off each glass with a splash of club soda. Garnish with a slice of lime and a sprig of mint.

# Sake Margaritas

You might not expect sake to step in for tequila so neatly, but this drink really hits the spot. You can dip the glass rim in a saucer of salt after rubbing it with a cut lime (as on page 116), but this also stands on its own without any garnish. Taste this mix, and if you'd like the drink a trifle sweeter, splash in a bit more Triple Sec.

1 cup sake (8 ounces)

½ cup fresh lime juice (from 7–10 large
    limes), plus an extra lime for garnish
    (optional; see headnote)

¼ cup Triple Sec (2 ounces)

2 cups ice

Salt, to coat the rims of the glasses
    (optional)

STRAIGHT UP: Shake all the ingredients except the extra lime and the salt in 2 batches in a martini shaker. Strain out the ice and pour into highball glasses.

BLENDED: Mix all the ingredients except the extra lime and the salt in a blender. Pour into highball glasses or shallow stemmed glasses and serve.

# White Peach Sangria ·

This sangria is fruity and refreshing without being too sweet. Good sangria depends on good fruit. Use luscious white Babcock peaches when they're in season. When peaches aren't perfect, use nectarines when they're at their peak.

For a party, you can easily double or triple this recipe. Fill a clear punch bowl to get the full effect of the peach and citrus slices and the sangria's beautiful color. You don't have to add ice if you chill the sangria very well before serving, but many people like sangria with ice.

5 white peaches, peeled; 3 cut into chunks
  and 2 cut into slices
2 tablespoons sugar
2 tablespoons water
1 bottle (750 ml) dry white wine

½ cup peach brandy
1 cup fresh orange juice
1 orange, sliced, with the peel left on
1 lime, sliced, with the peel left on
1–2 cups ice (optional)

In a blender, puree the peach chunks with the sugar and water. In a large pitcher (preferably a clear one), combine the wine, brandy, orange juice, peach puree, and the sliced orange, lime, and peaches. Add ice, if you like. Stir and mix well before serving.

# Fuji Apple, Walnut, and Dill Salad

You can play around with just about every ingredient in this recipe. Although I like the extra crispness of Fuji apples, if they aren't in season, use Granny Smith or Golden Delicious apples or even Bosc, Bartlett, or red pears (as long as they're sweet, juicy, and firm). The dressing is a good place to try gourmet vinegars. I've made this salad with late-harvest Riesling vinegar as well as blood orange vinegar, and both were delicious. Change the amount of the ingredients, adding more grapes or celery according to your taste, or use fresh orange juice (from the orange you zested) instead of lemon juice.

DRESSING

- 2 tablespoons rice wine vinegar
- 2 tablespoons almond oil, walnut oil, or extra-virgin olive oil
- 2 tablespoons plain low-fat yogurt
- 1 teaspoon Dijon mustard
- 1 tablespoon finely grated orange zest
- 2 teaspoons fresh lemon juice or orange juice
- 1/4 teaspoon kosher salt
- 1/4 teaspoon freshly ground black pepper

- 1 cup walnut pieces
- 2 cups chopped Fuji apples
- 2 tablespoons chopped fresh dill
- 1/4 cup thinly sliced celery hearts
- 1/2 cup seedless green grapes (left whole or halved)

- 3 Belgian endive leaves for garnish (optional)

FOR THE DRESSING: Combine all the ingredients in a small bowl. Set aside.

In a medium bowl, combine the walnuts, apples, dill, celery, and grapes.

Pour the dressing over the apple mixture and stir until blended. If you like, arrange the endive leaves in a triangle on a serving plate and mound the salad in the center. Refrigerate the salad before serving or serve right away.

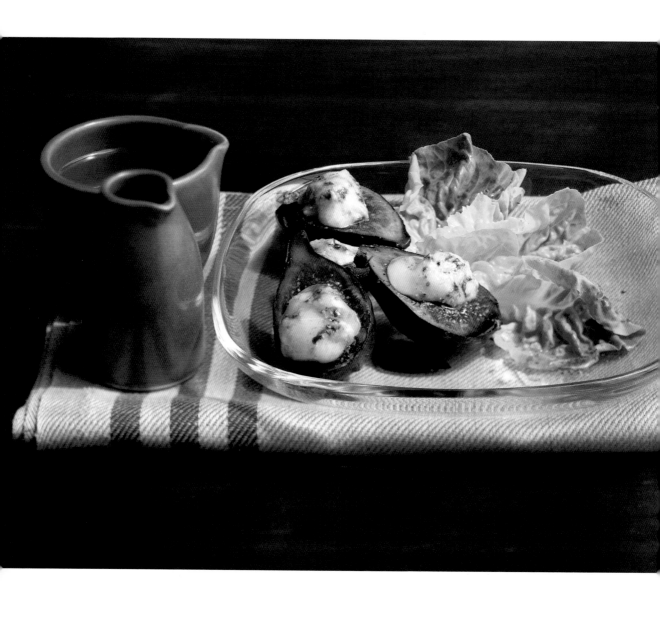

# Baby Greens and Figs Stuffed with Gorgonzola Cheese

SERVES 4

When figs are in season, the kids are in school, and the nights are cool again, I like to make this salad of figs stuffed with Gorgonzola. Don't stuff the figs ahead of time. Have your guests stuff them while you wash the greens. Then roast the figs briefly and serve up a gorgeous fall salad.

Want to host your own small fig festival? Serve these stuffed figs, Figs with Balsamic Reduction and Parmesan (page 177), and Fig, Nut, and Mushroom Pâté (page 182), along with a glass of Sancerre before dinner or a glass of Sauternes afterward.

8–10 ripe Black Mission figs
  About 8 tablespoons Gorgonzola cheese,
    plus extra for garnish (optional)
4 tablespoons top-quality balsamic vinegar
2 teaspoons sea salt, plus more for the
    greens

Freshly ground black pepper
3 cups mixed baby greens
Extra-virgin olive oil

Preheat the oven to 375°F.

Slice the figs in half. Into the fleshy center of each fig half, tuck about ½ tablespoon Gorgonzola. Arrange the fig halves on a baking sheet, cut side up, and sprinkle with 2 tablespoons of the vinegar, the 2 teaspoons salt, and pepper to taste. Set aside. (Don't put the figs into the oven until the greens are ready, because you want to add the figs to the greens while they're still warm.)

In a large bowl, toss the greens with a drizzle of olive oil, the remaining 2 tablespoons vinegar, and salt and pepper to taste. Arrange on individual plates.

Slide the baking sheet into the oven and cook the figs just until the cheese begins to melt, 2 to 3 minutes. Arrange the warm fig halves around the edge of each salad, allotting 4 or 5 per person. If you like, crumble a little Gorgonzola over the top of each salad before serving.

# Sunday Cheesesteak Sandwiches with Homemade Provolone Sauce

MAKES 4 BIG SANDWICHES

This is a regular treat at our house during football season. Yes, I know—it's an extravagance to use rib-eye, but because these steaks are better marbled than most steaks, they have the best flavor. For a traditional cheesesteak sandwich, you can slice the raw steak into ultra-thin slices and cook the slices in a hot pan. Because I don't want to miss the game, I sear the entire rib-eye and slice it thin after it's cooked.

6 tablespoons extra-virgin olive oil
1 green bell pepper, thinly sliced
1 red bell pepper, thinly sliced
1 cup thinly sliced mushrooms
1 large onion, cut into paper-thin slices
2 tablespoons chopped fresh oregano

1/2 teaspoon kosher salt
  Freshly ground black pepper
1 1/2 pounds rib-eye steak, about 1 inch thick
4 crusty hoagie rolls, sliced
  Homemade Provolone Sauce (recipe follows)

Cat's Note  If you want a traditionally cooked cheesesteak, wrap the rib-eye in plastic wrap and put it in the freezer for 30 minutes. Remove the steak from the freezer and cut it into very thin slices. Sauté the slices in olive oil with oregano, salt, and pepper.

Preheat the oven to 250°F.

Heat a large cast-iron skillet (or any heavy skillet) over medium-high heat. Add 3 tablespoons of the olive oil to the pan. Add the peppers and mushrooms and sauté until slightly softened, about 3 minutes. Add the onion and sauté until it's just the way you like it. Transfer the peppers, mushrooms, and onion to an ovenproof platter and place in the oven to keep warm.

Heat the remaining 3 tablespoons olive oil in the pan over medium-high heat. Add the oregano, salt, and pepper to taste and sauté quickly. As soon as the seasonings are hot, sauté the steak for 5 to 6 minutes. Turn the steak and cook for another 5 to 6 minutes for medium-rare.

Remove the steak from the pan, place on a cutting board, and let it rest for 5 minutes. Thinly slice the steak. With tongs, divide the meat among the hoagie rolls and top with the onion mixture. Spoon some of the cheese sauce over the meat and vegetables, cover with the top of the roll, and serve.

## Homemade Provolone Sauce

MAKES 2 CUPS

Slow, gentle heat is the key to a smooth, creamy cheese sauce.

1 tablespoon unsalted butter
1/2 pound provolone cheese, diced small
2 large egg yolks, beaten
1 tablespoon all-purpose flour

1 1/2 cups whole milk
Kosher salt and freshly ground black
  pepper

Half fill the bottom of a double boiler with water and place over medium heat. Melt the butter in the top of the double boiler. (If you don't have a double boiler, melt the butter in a stainless-steel bowl set snugly inside a saucepan filled with a few inches of water.) Add the cheese and let it soften slowly, stirring.

Meanwhile, in a medium bowl, whisk together the egg yolks, flour, and milk. When the cheese has melted, pour the egg mixture into the top of the double boiler and whisk until the sauce is warm and begins to thicken. Continue to cook over medium heat, whisking constantly. Add salt and pepper to taste. When the sauce is thick, turn the heat to low to keep it warm while you assemble the sandwiches. Use immediately. Cover and refrigerate any leftover sauce.

# Saffron Potato Omelet

If you have scallions and saffron on hand—and potatoes and onions in your pantry—this astonishingly good omelet is a mainstay for dinner, lunch, or brunch, without a trip to the grocery store. Or serve it with a variety of Spanish tapas, preferably late in the evening in front of a fire. Place it on a serving platter in the center of the table, surrounded with small plates of Serrano ham or manchego cheese and, of course, lots of olives and red wine.

5 tablespoons extra-virgin olive oil

1 teaspoon kosher salt

2 large onions, finely chopped

3 large russet (baking) potatoes (about 1 1/2 pounds)

1/4 teaspoon saffron threads

1/4 cup chicken stock

6 large eggs

1/2 cup thinly sliced scallions (about 5), plus more for garnish

1/8–1/4 teaspoon freshly ground black pepper

2 tablespoons chopped fresh flat-leaf parsley, for garnish

Pour 2 tablespoons of the olive oil into a 12-inch nonstick skillet over medium heat and add 1/2 teaspoon of the salt. Add the onions and cook, stirring occasionally, until golden, about 20 minutes. Transfer the onions to a large bowl and allow them to cool. Set the skillet aside.

While the onions are cooking, peel the potatoes and cut them into 1/2-inch cubes or half-moon-shaped slices. In a saucepan of boiling salted water, cook the potatoes until almost tender, about 8 minutes. Drain in a colander and let them cool. When the potatoes have cooled, add them to the bowl with the onions and stir to combine. (The onion-potato mixture can be made 1 day ahead and refrigerated, covered.)

Crumble the saffron threads into a small heatproof bowl. In a small saucepan, heat the chicken stock until hot but not boiling, then pour it over the saffron threads. Let the mixture steep for about 5 minutes.

In a large bowl, whisk together the eggs, scallions, saffron mixture, the remaining 1/2 teaspoon salt, and the pepper. (I add a lot of black pepper to this omelet, but start with a little and see what you prefer.) Add the onion-potato mixture and stir to combine.

Heat the remaining 3 tablespoons olive oil in the skillet over medium-high heat until hot but not smoking. Add the egg mixture, spreading the potatoes evenly across the pan. Reduce the heat to medium. Gently stir the eggs for about 1 minute, or until the omelet begins to set. Shift the skillet so that one quarter of the omelet is directly over the center of the burner and cook for 1 minute. Shift the skillet 3 more times, cooking each quarter of the omelet for 1 minute. Reduce the heat to low, center the skillet over the burner, and continue to cook until the omelet is almost set, about 4 minutes.

Slide the omelet, bottom side down, onto a baking sheet or a large heatproof platter, then invert it back into the skillet. Cook the second side of the omelet over low heat until golden, about 4 minutes, then slide the omelet onto a platter. Serve warm or at room temperature, garnished with the scallions and parsley. (The omelet can be made up to 24 hours ahead, covered, and refrigerated. Let it come to room temperature for 30 minutes before serving.)

# Crispy "Fried" Chicken

SERVES 4 TO 6

This chicken tastes fried but does away with all the grease. The secret is to lock in the moisture by dredging the chicken pieces in flour and dipping them into buttermilk that you've spiced up with paprika, cayenne, mustard, and sage. Then you roll the pieces in crushed cornflakes.

2 teaspoons extra-virgin olive oil
1 2½- to 3-pound fryer, cut into pieces
    (2 breasts, 2 thighs, 2 legs, 2 wings)
½ cup all-purpose flour
1 teaspoon kosher salt
¼ teaspoon freshly ground black pepper
2 cups cornflakes

½ cup light buttermilk
1 tablespoon Dijon mustard
⅛ teaspoon cayenne pepper (optional)
1 teaspoon paprika
½ tablespoon finely chopped fresh sage or
    ½ teaspoon ground sage

Preheat the oven to 425°F.

Pour the olive oil into a baking pan large enough to hold the chicken pieces in a single layer without crowding. Using your fingers, rub the oil over the dish so that it's completely but lightly coated.

Rinse the chicken in cold water and pat dry. In a wide bowl or on a large plate, season the flour with the salt and pepper. Dredge each chicken piece in the flour until it's completely coated. Tap the chicken against the side of the bowl to loosen any excess flour and set the pieces aside. Discard the flour.

Crush the cornflakes by placing them in a big resealable plastic bag, carefully pressing the bag to push out the air. Seal the bag (leaving as little air inside as possible) and crush the flakes using a rolling pin. Pour the crushed flakes into a wide bowl or onto a large plate.

In a bowl large enough to dip the chicken pieces, mix the buttermilk, mustard, cayenne (if using), paprika, and sage. Give each floured

Cat's Note   The younger the child, the fewer spices you'll need to add, because kids' palates are sensitive. For very small children, omit the spices entirely or add just a hint. If the kids eat it, you can try adding a little more spice the next time you make it.

chicken piece a good buttermilk bath all over, then roll in the crushed flakes.

Arrange the chicken pieces in the prepared baking pan. Bake for 15 to 20 minutes, lower the heat to 375°F, and bake for another 25 to 30 minutes, until cooked through and crispy. (The juices should run clear when the meat is pierced with a knife.) Serve.

# Rolling Sushi
# with Family and Friends

Sushi is fresh and healthy, but here's the main point about this dinner: you don't have to do all the work yourself. Sure, you can slice the ingredients beforehand and have the rice ready to go, but then bring it all to the table in bowls and let everyone roll their own.

First off, praise the sushi rolls your kids make, no matter how lumpy. You're setting your children up for a lifetime of cooking while helping them feel good about making their own dinner.

It's worth investing in little bamboo mats for rolling sushi, but if you don't have mats, use sheets of heavy-duty foil. Lay a sheet of plastic wrap over the bamboo mat or the foil. Place a sheet of nori (dried seaweed), smooth side down, on the plastic wrap. Run your hands under tap water and then, with wet hands, pat a layer of rice about 1/2 inch thick against the rough side of the nori square, covering it with an even layer of rice and leaving a thin border along the top and bottom. (The photo on page 102 gives you an idea of how this should look.)

Now you can either leave the roll as is, with the rice side up (in which case the rice will be on the inside of the sushi roll) or turn the nori square over so that the rice side is down (in which case the rice will be on the outside of the roll).

Spread your fillings on the nori square sparingly—don't overcrowd the roll—and align them in a narrow row along the side of the square that's closest to you. Then begin slowly rolling the bamboo mat or the foil away from you. (The plastic wrap helps keep the sushi nice and neat, but don't roll it up in the sushi.) Each time you roll, tighten the roll by pulling the mat or the foil toward you, then pull the front of the mat or the foil away from you and roll again. The nori sheet should be tight by the time you get to the end. Pull the plastic from the roll, lift the roll from the mat or the foil, and place it on a cutting board. Dip a sharp or serrated knife in water and slice the roll into rounds about 1 inch thick.

Place a small sushi plate in front of each guest and a tiny bowl or plate holding a knob of wasabi paste and a small pitcher of soy sauce (creamers work well). Have fun!

# The Zoran Roll

Who says sushi has to include raw fish? Named after my son, Zoran, this inside-out roll reinvents sushi. It's a great dish to serve to your vegetarian friends. Don't be daunted by rolling sushi. It's easy, honestly. Just follow my tips on page 130 and have fun.

I use English cucumber for sushi because it has fewer seeds. You can also use a regular cucumber. Just peel it, slice it in half lengthwise, and scoop out the seeds with a spoon, as shown on page 65.

4 sheets toasted nori (dried seaweed)

4 cups Sushi Rice (recipe follows)

2 tablespoons black sesame seeds (see note)

1 small red bell pepper, roasted (page 242), peeled, quartered, and sliced into thin strips

½ avocado, peeled, pitted, and sliced into eighths

12 kalamata olives, pitted and halved (see page 12)

¼ English cucumber or regular cucumber (see headnote, page 131), peeled and sliced into strips 2 inches by ⅛ inch

6 tablespoons crumbled feta cheese

Soy sauce and wasabi paste or Avocado Tzatziki (page 28)

Cover a bamboo mat with plastic wrap. Place a sheet of nori on top, smooth side down. With water-moistened hands, spread 1 cup of the rice evenly on top of the nori, leaving about a ¼-inch border at the top and bottom edges. Press firmly. Evenly sprinkle the rice with ½ tablespoon of the sesame seeds, pressing them gently into the rice with your fingers.

Leaving the plastic wrap in place on the mat, turn the nori sheet over so that the rice and the sesame seeds are facing down. (If this is difficult, put a new sheet of plastic wrap on top of the rice before flipping it.)

Arrange one quarter of the pepper, avocado, olives, cucumber, and feta on the nori in a neat, narrow row that aligns with the edge of the nori sheet closest to you. Roll the bamboo mat away from you (making sure not to roll the plastic wrap or the mat), pressing the ingredients inside the cylinder-shaped sushi. Give the bamboo mat one last final firm press with both hands to shape the sushi, then remove the mat and the plastic wrap. Place the sushi roll on a cutting board. Dip a sharp or serrated knife into water and slice the roll into rounds about 1 inch thick.

Repeat the process with the remaining ingredients. Serve with soy sauce and wasabi paste or with the tzatziki.

## Cat's Notes

To be sure your nori will be crisp, buy packages labeled toasted nori. Once you open the package, wrap the nori tightly in plastic wrap, and it will keep for months.

I love the look of black sesame seeds on sushi, but you can use regular sesame seeds here too. Don't buy too many sesame seeds at one time. Because of their high oil content, they turn rancid fast. Better to buy seeds in small amounts and use them fairly quickly. If you have trouble finding black sesame seeds, see Resources (page 245).

# Sushi Rice

You can make a sushi roll from practically any ingredients—as long as your rice is perfect.

2 cups short-grain or medium-grain white rice

3 cups cold water

4 tablespoons rice wine vinegar

1/2 teaspoon kosher salt

In a heavy, medium pan with a tight-fitting lid, combine the rice and water and set over high heat. As soon as the mixture comes to a boil, reduce the heat to low, cover the pan, and let the rice simmer for 20 minutes, or until the liquid is absorbed.

Transfer the rice to a large platter or bowl and slowly drizzle the vinegar over it while gently stirring. Add the salt and continue to stir until the rice reaches room temperature and becomes sticky.

As soon as the rice is cool enough to handle, start rolling the sushi, following any of the filling suggestions in this chapter or creating your own custom-made fillings.

Cat's Note  I cook rice in a pot, but if you have a rice cooker, go ahead and use it.

# Tropical Fruit and Jerk Chicken Sushi

You wouldn't expect seaweed to work with spiced chicken and mangoes, but this is a refreshing take on sushi. In Jamaica, jerk chicken is coated with a blend of chilies and spices, including thyme, allspice, nutmeg, and cinnamon. Although you can make your own jerk seasoning, it's much easier to buy a good blend, which you'll find in most grocery stores.

The Pickapeppa Sauce (also known as Jamaican ketchup), available in most specialty markets and many grocery stores, adds just the right touch. Pour a little into a small ramekin and see what you think of it.

2 boneless, skinless chicken breast halves

2 tablespoons jerk seasoning (see headnote)

1 teaspoon kosher salt

1/2 teaspoon freshly ground black pepper

2 tablespoons extra-virgin olive oil

4 sheets toasted nori (dried seaweed)

4 cups Sushi Rice (page 133)

2 tablespoons black or regular sesame seeds

1/2 mango, peeled, pitted, and sliced into strips

1/2 avocado, peeled, pitted, and sliced into strips

1/4 English cucumber, peeled and sliced into strips 2 inches by 1/8 inch

2 tablespoons pickled ginger

Pickapeppa Sauce (see headnote)

Rub the chicken breasts with the jerk seasoning, salt, and pepper. Pour the olive oil into a large skillet and place it over high heat. When the oil is almost smoking, add the chicken, reduce the heat to medium-high, and sear on both sides until the chicken is golden brown and thoroughly cooked, 3 to 4 minutes per side. Transfer the chicken to a cutting board to cool. When it's cool enough to handle, slice the chicken into 1/4-inch-thick strips and set aside.

Cover a bamboo mat with plastic wrap. Place a sheet of nori on top, smooth side down. With water-moistened hands, spread 1 cup of the rice evenly over the nori, leaving about a 1/4-inch border at the top and bottom edges. Press firmly. Sprinkle the rice with 1/2 tablespoon of the sesame seeds, pressing them gently into the rice with your fingers. Leaving the plastic wrap in place on the mat, turn the nori sheet over so that the rice and the sesame seeds are facing down.

Arrange one quarter of the chicken strips, mango, avocado, and cucumber on the nori in a neat, narrow row that aligns with the edge of the nori sheet closest to you. Roll the bamboo mat away from you (making sure the plastic wrap stays with the mat), pressing the ingredients inside the cylinder-shaped sushi. Press the bamboo mat firmly with both hands one final time to shape the sushi, then remove the mat and the plastic wrap. Place the sushi roll on a cutting board. Dip a sharp or serrated knife into water and slice the roll into rounds about 1 inch thick.

Repeat the process with the remaining ingredients. Serve with pickled ginger and Pickapeppa Sauce.

# Prosciutto, Pear, and Blue Cheese Sushi

This sushi combines the sharp creaminess of blue cheese with thin, succulent pear strips and rich, buttery prosciutto. It doesn't taste like any sushi you've tried, but when these flavors are rolled up in rice, they're just the right contrast of sweet and tart, juicy and creamy, and crisp and luscious.

3 tablespoons pine nuts

4 sheets toasted nori (dried seaweed)

4 cups Sushi Rice (page 133)

4 thin slices prosciutto

2 tablespoons crumbled good blue cheese (I like Point Reyes; see page 245)

½ ripe pear, peeled and sliced into 2-inch-wide strips

2 tablespoons Balsamic Reduction (page 240)

Cat's Note    Toast the pine nuts for just a few minutes on a small, dry baking sheet at 350°F. Shake the pan occasionally. As soon as you smell them, remove the pan from the oven.

Toast the pine nuts, and once they've cooled, transfer them to a resealable plastic bag. Before sealing, press the bag flat with your hands to expel most of the air. Roll a rolling pin or a full bottle of wine over the bag to crush the pine nuts. Set aside.

Cover a bamboo mat with plastic wrap. Place a sheet of nori on top, smooth side down. Moisten your hands. Spread 1 cup of the rice over the nori, leaving about a ¼-inch border at the top and bottom edges. Press firmly. Sprinkle the rice with ½ tablespoon of the pine nuts, pressing them gently into the rice with your fingers. Leaving the plastic wrap in place on the mat, turn the nori sheet over so that the rice and pine nuts are facing down.

Lay 1 prosciutto slice smoothly and neatly over the nori. Arrange one quarter of the blue cheese and the pear strips in a neat, narrow row that aligns with the edge of the nori sheet closest to you. Roll the bamboo mat away from you (making sure the plastic wrap stays with the mat), pressing the ingredients inside the cylinder-shaped sushi. Press the bamboo mat firmly with both hands one final time to shape the sushi, then remove the mat and the plastic wrap. Place the sushi roll on a cutting board. Repeat the process with the remaining ingredients to make 3 more rolls.

Dip a sharp or serrated knife into water and slice each roll into rounds 1 inch thick. Drizzle with the balsamic reduction, sprinkle with the remaining pine nuts, and serve.

# Rice

Rice is a mainstay for my family's dinners. I serve rice with everything from stew to fish and count on it for sushi dinners.

**Short-grain brown rice** is the kind I cook most often. It's more nutritious than white rice, and I've come to love its nutty flavor. It seems to have less starch than other varieties and has a very clean taste. I cook brown rice at least three or four times a week and have the pot in the fridge ready to warm up for lunch or dinner. Serve it with Curried Lentils with Butternut Squash (page 93).

**Short-grain or medium-grain white rice** is what I turn to when I make sushi—and we eat a lot of sushi at my house.

**Wild rice** is the "restaurant" rice I serve with Cornish game hen, duck breasts, chicken, or roast pork. It has the most full-bodied flavor and stands up well to dishes with sauces.

**Wild rice with wheat berries**, available in health-food stores, has all the flavor of a standard wild rice, but the texture of the wheat berries gives this some extra pizzazz and makes a dish seem a little fancier.

I use **Arborio rice** for all my risottos and when I make risotto balls stuffed with cheese or risotto cakes to serve with fish, seafood, and meats. Asparagus risotto and mushroom risotto make frequent appearances at my table during the winter. You can also use an Italian rice called **Carnaroli** for risottos, but I prefer the shorter-grained Arborio, because it cooks faster and has a softer texture. Many high-end grocery stores sell Arborio and Carnaroli rice.

# Chicken Potpie with Puff Pastry

The next time you roast a chicken for dinner, roast a bigger bird than you need. After dinner, take a few sheets of puff pastry out of the freezer, stash them in the fridge, and plan to make this vegetable-filled potpie the next day. No worries about rolling out dough: the puff pastry crust lets you put these cozy little pies together quickly. Put your family to work tracing out the pastry circles and capping the potpies.

Use 8- to 10-ounce ramekins if you have them. If you have only small ramekins, those work fine too—and they're especially nice for kids.

2 sheets puff pastry, thawed and refrigerated

2 cups chicken stock, homemade (pages
    231–233) or store-bought

8 thyme sprigs, plus 2 tablespoons chopped
    fresh thyme

4 tablespoons extra-virgin olive oil

1 medium onion, chopped

1 cup diced (¼ inch) carrots

1 cup sliced (¼ inch) celery

1 cup fresh or frozen peas (if frozen, don't
    thaw)

1 cup diced (¼ inch) zucchini

½ cup dry white wine

2 cups shredded roasted chicken (don't
    include skin)

    Kosher salt and freshly ground black
    pepper

3 tablespoons unsalted butter

3 tablespoons all-purpose flour

Place the ramekins on a baking sheet and set aside. Remove the pastry from the refrigerator and spread it out on a piece of parchment over a cool flat surface. Place one of the ramekins over the puff pastry and cut the pastry into the shape of the ramekin, leaving a 1-inch overhang all the way around. Place the pastry rounds on a plate, separated by parchment or plastic wrap, and cover with plastic wrap. Refrigerate until ready to use, for up to 24 hours.

Cat's Note   Potpies can be anything you want them to be. The standard veggies are carrots, celery, and onion, but you can add chopped spinach, tomatoes, mushrooms, bok choy, ginger, scallions, and even chunks of butternut squash. Don't be afraid to try something new. Just go with what you have and follow your instincts.

In a large pot, combine the stock and the thyme sprigs. Bring to a boil, cover, and reduce the heat to low. Let the stock cook for 15 to 30 minutes; remove and discard the thyme sprigs just before using the stock.

Meanwhile, pour 2 tablespoons of the olive oil into a large skillet and place over medium-high heat. Add the onion and sauté until translucent, 3 to 4 minutes. Add the carrots and celery and sauté for 2 to 3 minutes. (If the pan needs more oil, add the remaining 2 tablespoons olive oil.) Add the peas, zucchini, and chopped thyme. Sauté for 2 to 3 minutes, until the zucchini is just cooked.

Pour the wine over the vegetables and bring to a boil. Reduce the liquid by half. Remove the pan from the heat and stir in the chicken. Season to taste with salt and pepper and set aside.

In a large saucepan, melt the butter over medium heat. Slowly sprinkle in the flour, stirring constantly with a whisk or a wooden spoon until the butter and flour form a thick paste. Continue to stir until the mixture turns golden and begins to bubble slightly over medium to low heat. Immediately ladle $1/2$ cup of the hot stock into the flour mixture, whisking well to eliminate lumps. Increase the heat to medium-high and continue to whisk and incorporate the stock, $1/2$ cup at a time, until all the stock has been added and the sauce is bubbling and has thickened to the consistency of a thick soup. Remove from the heat. Taste and correct the seasoning, adding more salt and pepper if needed.

Preheat the oven to 400°F.

Pour the sauce over the chicken and vegetable mixture and gently combine with a wooden spoon. Fill each ramekin about three-quarters full with the mixture.

Remove the pastry rounds from the refrigerator and place 1 round on top of each ramekin. Press the overhanging inch of pastry firmly against the side of the ramekin all the way around.

Bake for 20 to 25 minutes, or until the pastry has puffed and turned golden brown. Serve immediately, but warn children that it's very hot.

# Salmon and Scallop Skewers with Romesco Sauce

SERVES 4

A specialty of the Catalan region of Spain, romesco sauce is a fragrant, garlicky blend of ground almonds, garlic, tomatoes, and peppers. The sauce changes from town to town, and the ingredients can include hazelnuts and various liquors. I like to make a very pure, simple romesco sauce that I can whip up in my blender.

Roasting the red pepper and tomatoes gives this sauce its deep flavor. If you do all the roasting the day before, the cooking takes just a few minutes once you thread the skewers. You can serve this sauce with any grilled fish. And it makes a terrific spread for bruschetta.

You can bake, grill, or broil the skewers.

3 tablespoons extra-virgin olive oil

Kosher salt and freshly ground black
pepper

3 tablespoons fresh lime juice

8 ounces salmon fillet (either 1 large piece
or several smaller pieces), cut into 8
equal chunks

8 sea scallops

8 8-inch wooden skewers, soaked in cool
water for at least 1 hour

1 red onion, cut into 1¼-inch chunks

1 red bell pepper, cut into 1¼-inch chunks

1 poblano chili, cut into 1¼-inch chunks

ROMESCO SAUCE

1 red bell pepper, roasted (see page 242),
peeled, seeded, and coarsely chopped

¼ cup cherry tomatoes, roasted (see page
241)

1 tablespoon coarsely chopped almonds (8 or
9 whole almonds)

2 garlic cloves, coarsely chopped

1 tablespoon sherry vinegar

¼ cup extra-virgin olive oil

Pinch of kosher salt

Freshly ground black pepper

Preheat the oven to 400°F or preheat the grill.

In a baking dish, combine the olive oil, salt and pepper to taste, and lime juice. Add the salmon and scallops to the dish and stir with a wooden spoon to coat all the pieces. Cover and refrigerate while you make the sauce.

FOR THE ROMESCO SAUCE: In a blender, combine the roasted pepper, tomatoes, almonds, garlic, vinegar, and olive oil, blending until smooth. (If you like, you can toss the whole almonds and garlic cloves into the blender, but I find that chopping them coarsely first prevents any large chunks from ending up stuck under the blender blades.) Season with salt and pepper to taste and set aside.

Remove the salmon and scallops from the marinade and discard the liquid. Pat dry each scallop and chunk of fish with paper towels. (If you don't dry each piece, they'll steam while cooking and have a soft exterior rather than a crisp one.)

Thread each skewer with 2 onion chunks, 1 salmon chunk, bell pepper and poblano chunks, and 1 scallop.

TO BAKE OR BROIL: Set the skewers on a baking sheet and place on the top rack of your oven. Bake or broil for 4 minutes, then rotate the baking sheet in the oven and give each skewer a half turn. Bake or broil for another 4 minutes, or until the salmon is firm to the touch and the scallops have begun to brown on the edges.

TO GRILL: These cook quickly, so it's best to set them to the side of the grill and not directly over a flame. Cook for 2 to 3 minutes, then turn. Turn the skewers gently so that the fish doesn't break and fall into the fire. When the salmon feels firm to the touch and the scallops show light grill marks, remove from the grill.

Arrange two skewers on each plate and spoon the sauce over them, or pile the skewers on a serving platter and serve the sauce in a bowl.

# Vegetable Couscous en Crépinettes

Otherwise known as "eat-your-veggies burritos," these are cute little bundles of cabbage and kale rolled around a filling of couscous and veggies. There's something about bundling food that makes it taste better—the vegetables inside these cabbage rolls are more tender and delicious than if they were sitting alone on your plate.

My mom made these all the time—she called them simply stuffed cabbage—but she varied the fillings so much that we never felt we were eating the same thing. I like this version because there's something to please everyone.

This is a "choose your fave" kind of dish. So as long as you end up with 2 cups of chopped vegetables, you can use anything: beets, carrots, summer squash, baby zucchini, broccoli, cauliflower—the list goes on and on. This is true for the herbs as well. Use what you have and what you know your family likes.

If you let the kids have a say in what goes inside and you put them to work rolling the crépinettes, they're more likely to eat them—and you'll make your dinner prep work a little easier.

Look for big heads of savoy cabbage, because the dainty little leaves on small heads are too small to wrap. You can use either the dinosaur or the curly variety of kale.

1½ tablespoons kosher salt

8 large savoy cabbage leaves

8 large kale leaves (see headnote)

2 cups chopped small carrots, baby squash, baby beets, baby zucchini, and/or cauliflower florets

1 cup raw couscous

2 tablespoons extra-virgin olive oil, plus ¼ cup

2 teaspoons **each** finely chopped fresh oregano, savory, and thyme

2 teaspoons kosher salt

1 teaspoon freshly ground black pepper

½ cup halved cherry tomatoes

2 tablespoons red wine vinegar

4 tablespoons (½ stick) unsalted butter

Feta-Mint Tzatziki (page 80; optional)

Harissa (available in specialty stores or see Resources, page 245; optional)

TO BLANCH THE CABBAGE AND KALE: Fill a large bowl (or the sink) half full of ice water.

Place a large pot half full of water over high heat and bring to a rolling boil. Add the salt. Add 3 or 4 cabbage leaves. When the water comes back to a boil, cook the leaves for 2 to 3 minutes, or until they have brightened in color and softened slightly. With a long-handled strainer, carefully and quickly remove the leaves from the hot water and transfer them to the ice water to stop the cooking process. When the water in the pot returns to a boil, add the remaining cabbage leaves and repeat the process. Repeat with the kale leaves. Remove the pot from the stove but leave the water in it.

Remove the leaves from the cold water and drain on a clean towel. Gently pat dry and set aside. Add more ice to the ice water.

Place the pot back on the stove over high heat. When the water returns to a boil, add the 2 cups of vegetables. After 2 to 3 minutes, when the vegetables are tender but their colors are still bright, remove them with a long-handled strainer or slotted spoon and plunge them directly into the ice water. Remove the vegetables from the ice water and drain on clean paper towels. Set aside.

**Cat's Note** As soon as you say anything along the lines of "Eat your veggies," kids tune out. Try the French name (unless your kids speak French, in which case you'll have to name these yourself).

TO COOK THE COUSCOUS: In a small saucepan, bring 2 cups water to a boil. Place the couscous in a medium bowl and pour the boiling water over it. Cover the bowl with a lid or a plate and let the couscous sit for 15 to 20 minutes, or until all the water has been absorbed. Toss the couscous with a fork to fluff it up, then add the 2 tablespoons olive oil, herbs, salt, and pepper and toss. Add the vegetables, cherry tomatoes, and vinegar and mix well.

TO ROLL UP THE LEAVES: Place 1 cabbage leaf on your work surface and smooth it flat. Place 1 kale leaf on top of the cabbage leaf, with the frilled edge hanging slightly over the bottom edge of the cabbage leaf (the edge closest to you). Place about ½ cup of the couscous mixture along the bottom third of the kale leaf (the side closest to you) and 1 inch in from each end. Roll the overlapping leaves away from you, folding them up firmly like a burrito and tucking the sides in. Set the finished bundle on a platter. Repeat with the remaining leaves and couscous mixture. Wrap each roll individually in plastic wrap and refrigerate for at least 1 hour, or until thoroughly chilled. (The rolls can be refrigerated for up to 24 hours.)

TO COOK THE CRÉPINETTES: Preheat the oven to 300°F.

Remove the rolls from the refrigerator and remove the plastic wrap. Place a large skillet over medium-high heat and add 2 tablespoons of the remaining olive oil and 1 tablespoon of the butter. When the oil and butter are hot, sear the rolls, 2 at a time, on all sides until lightly browned, 5 to 6 minutes. Transfer the rolls from the pan to an ovenproof platter and keep warm in the oven while you're searing the rest of the rolls. Add more oil and butter to the pan as needed.

To serve, top with a spoonful of tzatziki and a drizzle of harissa, if you like.

# Goat Cheese Fondue

To keep this fondue smooth and creamy, be sure to use an aged, firm goat cheese. Lavender sprigs add a subtle but interesting complement to the goat cheese, but they can be left out if you don't have any.

Of course you'll serve this with chunks of great bread, but don't stop there. Slices of crisp apple, broccoli florets, or your favorite vegetables—raw or blanched—are all fantastic dunked in this savory melted cheese sauce.

| | |
|---|---|
| 7 ounces well-aged, firm goat cheese | 2 tablespoons cognac |
| 8 ounces Gruyère or other Swiss cheese | 1/8 teaspoon freshly ground black pepper |
| 1 1/2 teaspoons cornstarch | 2 sprigs fresh lavender (optional) |
| 1 whole garlic clove, peeled | 1 pound artisan bread, sliced into large |
| 1 cup dry white wine | cubes for dunking |
| 1 teaspoon Dijon mustard | |

Grate both cheeses on a box grater or using the grater on your food processor. In a large bowl, combine the cheeses with the cornstarch, tossing well until completely mixed.

Cut the garlic clove in half and rub the cut sides thoroughly over the inside of your fondue pot, covering every inch.

Pour the wine into the fondue pot and place the pot on the stove over medium-low heat, watching carefully that it doesn't boil. When the wine is just beginning to simmer, add a small handful of cheese, stirring as it melts. Continue adding all the cheese slowly until the mixture is blended and smooth. Stir in the mustard, cognac, pepper, and lavender sprigs, if using. Whisk to bring the mixture together.

Carry the fondue pot to the table, and set it over a warming stand. Place baskets of bread chunks within easy reach for dipping.

# Grilled Watermelon and Shrimp

This is food for a party—bright, spicy, and fun. You'll most likely want to double this recipe for a group.

Take the do-it-yourself approach with serving this dish. Put out small bowls of lime wedges, toasted coconut, and chopped scallion and let your guests doctor their own. If you have some marmalade left over, you have the makings for a happy-hour appetizer the next evening. Just spread some goat cheese or cream cheese on toasted baguette slices and top with a spoonful of the marmalade.

SIMPLE SYRUP

  2 cups water

  1 cup sugar

SPICY PEPPER MARMALADE

  1 large red bell pepper, halved, seeded, and chopped

  1 jalapeño pepper, halved, seeded, and chopped

  1 tablespoon chopped fresh cilantro

  1/2 teaspoon finely grated lime zest

  2 tablespoons fresh lime juice

GRILLED WATERMELON AND SHRIMP

  6–8 8-inch wooden skewers, soaked in cool water for at least 1 hour (optional)

  1 small seedless watermelon

  1/4 cup extra-virgin olive oil

  Juice of 1 large lime, plus 4–5 juicy limes, cut into wedges, for garnish

  1/4 teaspoon cayenne pepper

  2 teaspoons chili powder

  1 teaspoon kosher salt

  1 teaspoon freshly ground black pepper

  1 pound jumbo or large shrimp (20–24), peeled and deveined, with the tail left on

  1/3 cup unsweetened shredded coconut, toasted (see note, page 155), for garnish

  1 scallion, sliced, for garnish

FOR THE SIMPLE SYRUP: Combine the water and sugar in a medium saucepan over high heat. Bring the mixture to a boil and stir until the sugar has dissolved completely. Remove from the heat. Pour 1/4 cup of the syrup into a heatproof measuring cup and set aside. You'll use this while grilling to baste the watermelon and give it nice grill marks.

FOR THE SPICY PEPPER MARMALADE: To the remaining syrup in the pan, add the bell pepper and jalapeño, mixing well. Simmer the mixture over medium heat for about 30 minutes, until it thickens. When the marmalade has the consistency of warm syrup, stir in the cilantro, lime zest, and lime juice. Place in a serving dish and set aside.

FOR THE GRILLED WATERMELON AND SHRIMP: Preheat the grill.

Cut the watermelon in half lengthwise and cut each half lengthwise so that you have 4 long quarters with the rind still on. Slice these crosswise into wedges about 1¹⁄₂ inches thick. Mix the reserved ¹⁄₄ cup simple syrup with 2 tablespoons of the olive oil and brush 8 of the best wedges from the center with the mixture. Put aside the remaining melon for another use.

In a large bowl, combine the remaining 2 tablespoons olive oil, lime juice, cayenne, chili powder, salt, and pepper. Toss in the shrimp and let marinate for 5 to 10 minutes. Thread 3 or 4 shrimp onto the wooden skewers, if using, or place the shrimp directly on the grill. Grill the shrimp just until they're pink and cooked through and show nice

grill marks, no more than 1½ minutes on each side. Do not overcook them: when they're pink, they're done.

Remove the shrimp from the grill and place on a large serving platter. Sear the watermelon slices for no more than 1 minute on each side, brushing on one more coat of the syrup during grilling. Arrange the grilled watermelon on the platter beside the shrimp. Set out small bowls of lime wedges, shredded coconut, and chopped scallion for garnish. Have your guests place 2 grilled watermelon slices on their plate with a few shrimp on top, squeeze a little fresh lime juice over both, and top with a spoonful of the marmalade and a bit of coconut and scallion.

Cat's Note   Toasting coconut is simple. Start with shredded or shaved coconut, which can be found in the bulk aisle of stores such as Whole Foods. Preheat the oven to 300°F. Spread 1 to 3 cups coconut on a baking sheet and bake for about 3 minutes. Turn the coconut with a spatula, rotate the baking sheet, and bake for another minute or two. Remove the sheet from the oven as soon as the coconut begins to turn golden.

# Crepe Party

Don't wait for Bastille Day to throw a crepe party. Any time you
need a little change of pace, make crepes and set out a variety
of fillings so your guests can spoon on their favorites. Crepes
can be filled with just about anything. You'll find some ideas on
the next pages.

A little roasted chicken, small bits of steamed broccoli, and
some grated cheddar cheese and voilà! chicken divan crepes. Or
fill a crepe with ham and cheddar or prosciutto, feta, and
kalamata olives. For dessert there's the classic belle Hélène
(sliced pear and dark chocolate) or fresh strawberries with
whipped cream or Nutella with slices of banana.

You have leeway with crepe folding too. Some people fold
crepes like an omelet, some fold them into quarters, and others
do a three-fold lengthwise. In Brittany, cooks often don't fold
the crepe at all but serve it open-faced with the "filling" piled
on top. However you do it, crepes can dress up ordinary
ingredients.

# Basic Crepes

Making crepes is like learning how to use a yo-yo—it takes a little practice before you get the hang of it. Once you know how to do it, though, you've got it for good.

A 6-inch crepe pan works well, but you can also make crepes in a heavy skillet. The batter should be light and very thin—much thinner than pancake batter. Resist the temptation to make the batter thicker by adding more flour. Thick batter turns into rubbery crepes.

½ cup all-purpose flour

1 large egg, beaten

1 cup milk

3 tablespoons melted unsalted butter for brushing the crepe pan

Preheat the oven to 250°F.

In a large bowl, whisk together the flour, egg, and milk until smooth. Place a 6-inch nonstick crepe pan, a heavy skillet, or a griddle over medium-high heat. (A nonstick pan is easiest.) Brush the pan lightly with the butter and wipe out any excess with a paper towel.

Pour in just enough batter (less than ¼ cup) to cover the bottom of the pan. Holding the pan by the handle, tilt it so that the batter runs across the bottom and covers the entire base of the pan. After about 1 minute, when the crepe turns golden brown and the edges brown and pull away from the pan, turn the crepe over and cook for 30 seconds, until the second side is lightly browned. Remove the crepe from the pan and place it on an ovenproof plate to cool. As the crepes cool, you can form a crepe stack and keep them warm in the oven. Repeat with the remaining melted butter and batter.

Serve the crepes immediately, or store in the freezer by placing sheets of wax paper or plastic wrap between them, then wrapping the entire batch in plastic wrap.

# Wild Mushroom
# and Kasseri Crepes

Whether you use chanterelles or substitute cremini or brown mushrooms isn't as important as using the prettiest, best mushrooms you can find. Just about any mushroom goes well with Greek kasseri cheese, which many grocery stores now offer. And if you can't find kasseri, use Parmesan.

You can make crepes on a griddle or in a seasoned skillet or a nonstick pan. Nonstick pans are easiest.

2 tablespoons unsalted butter
1 teaspoon extra-virgin olive oil
1½ cups finely chopped onion (about 1 large onion)
2 cups sliced chanterelle mushrooms (or substitute cremini or brown mushrooms)
10–12 crepes (page 157)
1 cup grated kasseri or Parmesan cheese

In a medium skillet or crepe pan or on a griddle, heat the butter and olive oil. When the butter is melted, add the onion. Cook until it is translucent, 2 to 3 minutes, then add the mushrooms and sauté until golden brown, 3 to 4 minutes. Remove the mixture from the pan, place in a small bowl, and set aside until you're ready to serve the crepes.

To fill the crepes, spoon a few tablespoons of the mushroom filling onto a crepe and sprinkle on about 1 tablespoon of the cheese, or enough to cover the crepe evenly. Fold the crepe over and place in a clean, dry skillet. Turn the heat to low and heat the crepe until the cheese begins to melt. Remove the crepe with a spatula and serve immediately.

# To-Die-For Garlic Mashed Potatoes

I am my father's daughter, and my father lives by the rule that occasionally you pull out all the stops and eat exactly what your heart desires. These heavenly mashed potatoes are extra rich, extra creamy, and totally irresistible.

3 teaspoons kosher salt

6 large russet (baking) potatoes

8 tablespoons (1 stick) unsalted butter, plus
    4 tablespoons

4 garlic cloves, minced

1 cup milk

1 cup heavy cream

Freshly ground black pepper

Put a large pot of water on to boil and add 2 teaspoons of the salt. Peel the potatoes and cut them into 1-inch cubes. When the water is boiling, add the potatoes and cook until fork-tender, 10 to 12 minutes.

While the potatoes are cooking, heat the 8 tablespoons butter in a medium skillet. When the butter is melted, add the garlic. Cook over low heat just until the garlic starts to color. Do not burn the butter. Take the pan off the heat and set aside to cool.

When the potatoes are easily pierced with a fork, drain them and return them to the pot; the residual heat will help the excess water evaporate. Mash the potatoes with a potato masher or a ricer. Gradually add the milk and cream while mashing until the potatoes are the desired consistency. Stir in the garlic mixture, add the remaining 1 teaspoon salt, and serve warm with the remaining 4 tablespoons butter and the pepper on the table.

# Creamed Pearl Onions and Peanuts

I love the shape of pearl onions, and this is the perfect dish to show them off. Using milk instead of cream creates a very light sauce, and a sprinkling of chopped peanuts adds a little crunch. This dish is about as southern as it gets.

You can substitute small, flat-topped cipollini onions, if you like.

| | |
|---|---|
| 2 cups fresh or frozen pearl onions (1³⁄₄ pounds) | 1 teaspoon kosher salt |
| 1 tablespoon unsalted butter | ¹⁄₂ teaspoon freshly ground black pepper |
| 1 tablespoon all-purpose flour | ¹⁄₄ teaspoon freshly grated nutmeg |
| 1 cup milk | 1 tablespoon chopped fresh thyme |
| | 2 tablespoons chopped roasted peanuts |

FOR FRESH ONIONS: Fill a large saucepan with water and set over high heat. When the water comes to a boil, blanch the onions for 2 minutes. Drain the onions in a colander and let them cool for a good 10 minutes before handling them. Peel the onions and set aside.

FOR FROZEN ONIONS: Remove the onions from their package, place in a small bowl, and let them sit for 20 minutes or so. Then add them to the sauce as directed. You can also take the onions out of the freezer the night before and keep them in the refrigerator. They'll be thawed by the time your sauce is ready.

Melt the butter in a small saucepan over low heat. Add the flour, whisking well, and cook for 2 to 3 minutes, allowing the mixture to bubble slightly but not brown.

Gradually add the milk, stirring constantly until creamy. Add the salt, pepper, nutmeg, and thyme and cook to reduce, 3 to 5 minutes.

When the sauce is a creamy but light consistency, add the onions and simmer for 5 more minutes. Spoon the creamed onions into a serving bowl and sprinkle with the chopped peanuts.

## Grilled Vegetables with Orange Mayo

SERVES 6 TO 8

ORANGE MAYO

> 3 juicy tangelos, tangerines, mandarins,
>    clementines, or blood oranges
> Store-bought mayonnaise
> Cayenne pepper (optional)
> Kosher salt (optional)

Cut the tangelos in half. Holding one at a time over a small saucepan, squeeze all the juice from 5 of the halves into the pan. Use a fork to press against the citrus to get out every drop of juice. Squeeze the last tangelo half over the pan, but leave some juice in it. Set that half aside and place the pan over high heat. When the juice begins to boil, lower the heat to medium-high and reduce the juice until it's thick and syrupy, taking care not to let it burn.

Pour the syrup into a small bowl and let it cool for 10 to 20 minutes. When the syrup is cool, add a scoop of mayonnaise to the bowl and whisk until smooth. Then whisk in just a little more fresh juice from the reserved half. Taste the mayo. If the flavor isn't bright enough, add a little more juice. If you like, finish with a pinch of cayenne and salt, or serve as is.

We have more varieties of oranges available to us in this country than ever before. Try Cara Cara oranges, also known as red navel oranges, which are available in specialty markets during the winter months and have raspberry-pink flesh. Blood oranges are a dark purply red. The tangelo, a cross between a mandarin orange and a grapefruit, is slightly tart and very fresh-smelling.

I reduce the tangelo juice and use it to make a fruity, fragrant mayo for grilled vegetables. It's amazing what a citrus-juice reduction does for ordinary store-bought mayo (and the mayo keeps in your fridge for 2 weeks).

3 crookneck squash

1 medium eggplant

2 large fennel bulbs or 3 medium bulbs

3 baby zucchini

   Extra-virgin olive oil

   Kosher salt

   Freshly ground black pepper

Preheat the grill.

Cut the vegetables in half lengthwise and rub sparingly all over with the olive oil. Sprinkle lightly with salt and pepper and place on the grill, cut side down. Grill for 4 to 6 minutes if the vegetables are small and for 5 to 8 minutes if they're large. Turn them so that the skin side is down and cook for 1 to 2 minutes, or until the vegetables are still firm but can be cut through easily with a knife. Remove from the grill and arrange the vegetables on a serving platter.

Spoon the mayo into a nice serving bowl and pass it around the table.

# Lemonade Cookies /

It's like a magic trick to pull a can of lemonade out of the freezer and say to the kids, "Do you think we can make this lemonade into cookies?"

If you want to make the cookie dough ahead of time, it can be refrigerated for several days if you seal it in two layers of plastic wrap. Dough straight from the refrigerator should bake for about 12 minutes; dough at room temperature bakes in 8 to 10 minutes.

| | |
|---|---|
| 1 6-ounce can frozen lemonade concentrate | 2 large eggs |
| $1/2$ pound (2 sticks) unsalted butter, softened | $2^1/2$ cups all-purpose flour |
| 1 cup sugar, plus extra to sprinkle over the cookies | 1 teaspoon baking soda |
| | $1/8$ teaspoon salt |
| 2 teaspoons finely grated lemon zest (optional) | |

Preheat the oven to 375°F.

Fill a large bowl with warm water and plop in the unopened can of lemonade to thaw while you mix the cookie dough.

In a large bowl, cream together the butter and sugar with a hand mixer. Add the lemon zest, if desired. Add the eggs one at a time, beating well after each addition. Continue beating until the mixture is light and creamy, 4 to 5 minutes, then set aside. In a separate bowl, whisk together the flour, baking soda, and salt.

Measure out $1/2$ cup of the thawed lemonade and set the rest aside. Add about one third of the flour mixture to the creamed butter and sugar. Stir, then add about one third of the $1/2$ cup lemonade. Continue adding the flour and lemonade alternately, stirring after each addition, until the mixture shows no streaks of flour. Beat on low speed with the mixer just until all the ingredients are combined.

Drop rounded teaspoonfuls of the dough 2 inches apart on an ungreased baking sheet.

Bake the cookies, checking them after 8 minutes. When the edges are just starting to brown, remove the cookies from the oven. (The centers will still look soft.) Using a pastry brush, immediately brush the top of each cookie very lightly with a little of the remaining lemonade concentrate, then lightly sprinkle with sugar. Transfer the cookies to a rack and allow them to cool completely.

# Lemon, Butter, and Sugar Crepes

MAKES 10 TO 12 CREPES

A crepe with a squeeze of fresh lemon juice and a dusting of sugar couldn't be simpler or more satisfying. These crepes remind me of the little crepe stands scattered throughout Paris. The sweeter the lemon, the better the crepes, so choose Meyer lemons, if available.

10–12 crepes (page 157)
    2 tablespoons unsalted butter
  5–6 fresh lemons, cut in half ($\frac{1}{2}$ lemon per crepe)
  $\frac{1}{4}$ cup sugar
  $\frac{1}{4}$ cup confectioners' sugar (optional)
   20 strawberries, sliced (optional)

Reheat the crepes one at a time in a large nonstick skillet. When the crepe is hot, put $\frac{1}{2}$ teaspoon of the butter on a knife and gently rub it over the crepe. Squeeze the juice from $\frac{1}{2}$ lemon over the crepe, sprinkle 1 teaspoon of the sugar sparingly over the juice, then fold the crepe in half and in half again to form a quarter circle.

If you like, dust a little confectioners' sugar on top and garnish with a few strawberry slices.

OPTION 1: Grand Marnier Crepes

MAKES 4 CREPES

The queen of crepes, this simple but impressive version calls for strawberries to be flamed in a mixture of butter and Grand

Marnier. Add the liqueur to the hot pan carefully, because it will flame up: keep the kids away from the stove, keep your hair pulled out of the way, and be ready to stand back.

4 crepes (page 157)

$^1/_2$ pint strawberries, hulled and sliced

2 tablespoons finely grated orange zest

1 teaspoon unsalted butter

$^1/_2$ cup Grand Marnier or other orange-flavored liqueur

4 tablespoons sugar

Whipped cream (optional)

Fold each crepe in half and in half again to form quarter circles. Arrange the folded crepes on a platter and set aside.

Put the berries in a small bowl and stir in the zest.

Place a large skillet over high heat. Add the butter, then the strawberries. Cook for 1 minute, then carefully add the Grand Marnier (see above). Be cautious, as the heat will cause the alcohol to ignite. Let the alcohol burn off, then remove from the heat.

Sprinkle the sugar over the strawberries and toss until well blended. Spoon the strawberries over the crepes and add several spoonfuls of whipped cream on one side of the platter, if you like. Serve immediately.

OPTION 2: Chocolate Crepes

MAKES 4 CREPES

The finer the chocolate in these crepes, the better the result. I like to use dark chocolate, such as El Rey or Scharffen Berger, but milk chocolate works too. (See Resources, page 245.)

1 tablespoon unsalted butter

6 ounces dark or milk chocolate

4 crepes (page 157)

$^3/_4$ cup whipped cream (optional)

Add the butter and chocolate to the top of a double boiler and set it over medium-high heat. (If you don't have a double boiler, set a stainless-steel bowl in a saucepan filled with a few inches of water.) As soon as the water begins to simmer, turn down the heat. Melt the butter and chocolate together, whisking until smooth. Do not let any water fly up into the chocolate, or the chocolate will seize, or become lumpy and harden.

Center a crepe on a serving plate. Spoon on one quarter of the chocolate mixture, then fold the crepe in half and in half again to form a quarter circle. Top with whipped cream, if desired, and serve.

# Chocolate Budino

*Budino* in Italian means pudding, but this is more like a molten cake, moist and almost gooey in the middle when served warm from the oven. I like to serve the budino with a scoop of homemade Banana Chocolate-Chunk Ice Cream (page 172), but it's also great with crème anglaise and fresh raspberries or strawberries. I use Callebaut or El Rey chocolate for this dessert (see Resources, page 245), but any premium chocolate will work.

½ pound high-quality bittersweet chocolate

3 large eggs, plus 3 large yolks

½ cup sugar

3 tablespoons all-purpose flour

12 tablespoons (1½ sticks) unsalted butter, softened

Place a rack in the middle of the oven and preheat the oven to 350°F.

Grease or spray a 9-inch cake pan or 12-cup muffin tin with vegetable or canola oil. Wipe out the excess oil with a paper towel. Set aside.

Grate the chocolate or chop it into small shards with a chef's knife or a serrated knife. (It's easier if you begin at a corner, particularly if the chocolate is very thick. Take it slowly and keep your fingers safe.) Place the chocolate in the top of a double boiler or a large bowl set over a saucepan of simmering water over very low heat. Melt the chocolate slowly, stirring occasionally.

In a medium bowl, gently whisk together the eggs, egg yolks, sugar, and flour. Mix until all the ingredients are well incorporated.

When the chocolate is smooth, remove the bowl from the hot water and add the butter. Stir until the butter is melted and the chocolate is smooth again. Add the egg mixture, mixing well.

Spoon the batter into the cake pan or the prepared muffin tin, filling each cup half full. Bake for 18 to 20 minutes in a cake pan or 11 to 12 minutes in a muffin tin. The edges will have just begun to pull away from the pan, and the center should still look moist and shiny. Remove the pan from the oven and let cool for 10 minutes.

While the pan is still warm, place a baking sheet over the top and invert the pan. Carefully lift the pan to release the cake. Transfer the cake to a serving platter or individual dessert plates if you've baked the cakes in a muffin tin. The budino is best if served warm but is also delicious at room temperature.

# Banana Chocolate-Chunk Ice Cream

The beauty of making your own chocolate-chunk ice cream is you get to decide how big you want the chunks. I tend to chop mine fairly fine, because I think you can taste the chocolate better that way, but if you like yours in larger pieces, go for it. Chocoholics, feel free to toss in a little more chocolate than is called for here; this recipe can take it.

If you're using an electric ice-cream maker, place the sleeve in the freezer overnight before using it. It must be completely frozen before you begin.

| | |
|---|---|
| 1 cup heavy cream | 2 egg yolks |
| 2 cups milk | 1/2 cup chopped banana |
| 1 cup sugar | 1/2 cup chopped dark chocolate |
| 1 vanilla bean, split (see page 95) | |

In a heavy-bottomed saucepan, combine the cream, milk, and sugar. Scrape the seeds of the vanilla bean into the cream mixture and then drop in the seedpod as well. Place the saucepan over medium-high heat. As soon as the mixture begins to boil, remove the pan from the heat.

Beat the egg yolks in a small bowl and slowly, in a very thin stream, add 1 cup of the hot cream mixture, stirring constantly to prevent the cream from "scrambling" the egg yolks. Gradually pour the yolk and cream mixture back into the saucepan, stirring constantly. Cook over medium heat for 8 to 10 minutes, stirring constantly, until the mixture begins to thicken slightly, coats the back of a spoon, and reaches 210°F on an instant-read thermometer.

Remove the pan from the heat. Pour the cream mixture through a fine-mesh strainer into a large bowl and let cool for 10 to 20 minutes. Cover and chill in the refrigerator for 2 to 3 hours. To speed the cooling process, you can rest the bowl in an ice bath: fill a larger bowl one third of the way with ice and cold water and place the bowl with the cream mixture into the ice-water bath. Stir the mixture occasionally until it is thoroughly chilled, about 20 minutes.

Follow the manufacturer's instructions for your ice-cream maker. Pour in the chilled cream mixture and let the machine churn for 20 to 25 minutes. Add the banana and

chocolate when the ice cream is three-quarters frozen. Let the machine churn for another 5 to 10 minutes max. Cover the surface of the ice cream with wax paper or plastic wrap before storing in the freezer to prevent ice crystals from forming.

Mix some decadent

and simple ingredients

with a few chef's tricks,

and you have

fabulous meals

for special evenings.

# Pheno

menai

## Appetizers

COOKING WITHOUT MEASURING:
**Figs with Balsamic Reduction
and Parmesan   177**

**Olive Panna Cotta
with Tomato "Raisins"   179**

**Fig, Nut, and Mushroom Pâté   182**

## Drinks

**Mango Margaritas   184**

**Easy Mint Juleps   186**

## Soups and Salads

**Farmers' Market Tomato
and Sweet Onion Soup   187**

**Potato–Celery Root Soup   188**

**Celery Root and Asian Pear Salad   190**

**Baby Greens with Prosciutto-Wrapped Apricots
and Sheep's Cheese   194**

## Main Dishes

**Salmon Fillets with Fava Bean Sauce   197**

**Oven-Roasted Crab Buon Natale   200**

**Balsamic-Glazed Duck Breast with Pear, Pearl Onion,
and Mushroom Hash   205**

**Pomegranate-Glazed Cornish Hens with Wild Rice
and Chestnut Stuffing   207**

**Porchetta   210**

**Basque Beef Tenderloin   213**

**Lamb Navarin   216**

## Side Dishes

**Glazed Baby Carrots and Fresh Dill   219**

**Blanched Chard   220**

## Desserts

**Alma's Italian Cream Cake   221**

**Hazelnut Chocolate Crème Brûlée   224**

**Custard Ice Cream   227**

# Phenomenal

# Figs with Balsamic Reduction and Parmesan

Fresh figs
1 chunk Parmesan cheese, preferably
    Parmigiano-Reggiano
Balsamic Reduction (page 240)

Allow 3 or 4 figs per person, depending on the size of the figs. With a vegetable peeler or a cheese slicer, shave the Parmesan into thin strips and set aside. Slice each fig in half and arrange the halves, cut side up, on individual plates. Drizzle the balsamic reduction over the fig halves and scatter the cheese over the figs and around the edge of the plate.

This preparation couldn't be easier. You just reduce balsamic vinegar into a syrup, then cut fresh, perfect figs in half, arrange them on a plate, drizzle on the balsamic reduction, and top with shavings of Parmesan. It's hard to believe something this simple could be so good.

Try this with ripe, juicy summer apricots too, or with plump, moist dates.

# Olive Panna Cotta with Tomato "Raisins"

SERVES 6

I love the silkiness of panna cotta and decided to try an unsweetened version of this Italian custard with cheese and olives. Turns out panna cotta makes a wonderful appetizer, especially when served with cherry tomato "raisins" and thin triangles of hearty toasted bread. This cream-colored panna cotta is satiny in texture, the subtle cheese counterpointed by intense hits of flavor from the dark chunks of olive. You can enjoy this appetizer year-round.

¼ cup chopped pitted kalamata olives (see page 12)
⅓ cup skim milk
1 envelope unflavored gelatin

2½ cups heavy cream
¼ cup grated kasseri or Parmesan cheese
Tomato "Raisins" (recipe follows)

Distribute the olives evenly among six 5-ounce ramekins and set aside.

Pour the milk into a small bowl and add the gelatin, stirring to dissolve. In a medium saucepan, heat the cream just to the boiling point. When small bubbles begin to form, slowly pour in the gelatin mixture. Whisk well until dissolved. Stir in the cheese and remove from the heat.

Pour the mixture into the ramekins, filling each one about three-quarters full. Cool to room temperature, then cover with plastic wrap and refrigerate overnight. Garnish with tomato "raisins" and serve.

# Tomato "Raisins"

Although I created these for the Olive Panna Cotta, I have since found so many other ways to serve them: on antipasto platters, alongside scrambled eggs for breakfast, tossed on top of salads or bruschetta, in pastas, or as a garnish for main courses.

1 pint cherry tomatoes, stems left on
2 tablespoons extra-virgin olive oil
1 teaspoon sea salt

Preheat the oven to 400°F.

Toss the tomatoes with the olive oil and salt and spread them on a baking sheet. Roast for 15 to 20 minutes, or until soft and wrinkly. Halfway through roasting, give the pan a good shake to turn the tomatoes. Remove the baking sheet from the oven and let the tomatoes cool. If you're not using them right way, transfer to a bowl, cover, and refrigerate. Serve chilled or let them come to room temperature for 20 minutes before serving.

# Figs

My earliest memory of figs was the colossal tree in the backyard of an elderly Greek neighbor who let my brothers and me play on his property when we lived in Mississippi. When I stood under that tree gazing up, the ripe figs looked like water balloons, full to bursting and ready to drop at the slightest breeze. We picked the ripe fruit from the lowest branches, pulling up our T-shirts to use as makeshift baskets, and gorged ourselves until our stomachs hurt. I learned early on to get out of the way when my brothers shook the branches.

That was my first close-up view of ripe figs, and I've learned over the years how to tell when a fig is perfectly ripe. Follow your sense of touch. The density of the fig will tell you whether it is ripe and full of juice and flavor. A ripe fig will give gently when you apply a light pressure with your fingertips and will have a sweet aroma. When you buy ripe figs, use them within a day or two; they won't keep any longer than that.

It's best to buy figs ripe, but if you have figs that aren't yet ripe, leave them on a windowsill or countertop and they'll ripen slightly in a day or two.

The five types of figs you'll see most often in the markets are the yellow-green Adriatic, the amber-colored Kadota, the rich, sweet Celeste (most often found in preserves), the soft brown Calimyrna, or Smyrna, and my favorite, Black Mission figs, named for the missionaries who planted the trees throughout California—and the ones hanging from that enormous tree in Mississippi. These were the first figs I tasted when I came to my home in California. I love the Mission for its honey flavor and for the contrast between its purple-black skin and its red flesh.

Don't worry too much about the variety of fig, though. As long as they're ripe, figs can be used interchangeably. When you see plump, dense, sweet-smelling, ready-to-burst figs, snap them up and bring them home to roast for salads (page 121), wrap into prosciutto (page 194), or slow-cook (page 243) and savor when the all-too-short fig season is over.

# Fig, Nut, and Mushroom Pâté

Slow-cooked figs are the heart and soul of this luxurious pâté. It tastes decadent and is perfect for your vegetarian friends. I love the balsamic syrup, but drizzle it on with a light hand—too much syrup and you lose the flavor of the figs.

You'll need to soak the seeds and nuts ahead of time—set them out to soak either overnight or in the morning before you leave for work.

| | |
|---|---|
| ½ cup raw pumpkin seeds | 4–6 Slow-Cooked Figs (page 243), halved, or store-bought dried figs |
| ½ cup shelled raw pistachios | |
| 1 cup balsamic vinegar | 2 tablespoons chopped fresh basil, plus extra leaves for garnish |
| ¼ cup extra-virgin olive oil, plus 2 tablespoons | |
| | 1 scallion, finely chopped |
| ½ small red onion, finely chopped | 1 teaspoon kosher salt |
| ½ cup quartered shiitake mushrooms | ½ teaspoon freshly ground black pepper |
| ¾ cup marsala | Pita chips or crackers |

In a medium bowl, cover the pumpkin seeds and pistachios with water and let soak for about 6 hours. Drain, rinse, and drain again.

In a small, heavy-bottomed pan, reduce the vinegar over medium heat until syrupy, 15 to 20 minutes. Set aside to cool.

Meanwhile, in a large skillet, heat the ¼ cup olive oil over high heat. Add the onion, reduce the heat slightly, and sauté just to bring out the flavor, about 2 minutes. Add the mushrooms and sauté, stirring constantly, until the onion is browned. Remove from the heat.

Pour the marsala into a small pan, add the figs, and set it over low heat. Rehydrate the figs by letting them warm slowly for 5 to 10 minutes. Drain, reserving both the figs and the marsala separately.

Put the pumpkin seeds, pistachios, the remaining 2 tablespoons olive oil, the mushroom mixture, basil, scallion, salt, pepper, and 2 tablespoons of the reserved marsala in a food processor. Process, scraping down the sides of the bowl, until the mixture is smooth. Taste and adjust the seasonings, adding more salt and pepper if needed.

Spoon the pâté into a serving bowl, top with the figs and a light drizzle of the balsamic syrup, and garnish with basil leaves. Serve with pita chips or crackers.

# Entertaining Vegetarians

Everyone needs a few good vegetarian recipes to serve guests who don't eat meat. Baby Greens and Figs Stuffed with Gorgonzola Cheese (page 121), Orange, Fennel, and Olive Salad (page 12), and the decadent Fig, Nut, and Mushroom Pâté (page 182) impress vegetarians and meat-eaters alike.

What do you do if a friend brings along a friend who's a vegetarian and you're serving meat for dinner? This calls for a shift in perspective. Make your salad the primary course and bulk it up with vegetables such as green beans, yellow and red bell peppers, and sprouts as well as canned chickpeas or pinto beans. I keep the ingredients for my zesty Three-Bean Salad with Fresh Mint (page 43) in my cupboard and my freezer, ready to be tossed together and served in just a few minutes. Make the meat a side dish and put together something quick but richly satisfying, like Orzo with Asiago Cheese (page 45) or Watermelon, Lime, Cashews, and Coconut (page 57). Go with what you have on hand, maybe substituting cantaloupe or fresh peach slices for the watermelon and setting out small ramekins of chopped mint and honey as your condiments. Look at your fruit bowl, your fresh herbs, and your spice cabinet and be creative.

# Mango Margaritas·

Luscious color and flavor make this one of my favorite margaritas. For tips on cutting fresh mangoes into chunks, see page 61.

1 1/2 cups cubed mango (about 4 large mangoes)
3/4 cup tequila
1/2 cup Triple Sec
1/2 cup fresh lime juice (from 7–10 large limes);
     reserve 4 thin slices of lime for garnish
4 cups crushed ice
2 tablespoons superfine sugar
4 mango chunks, peel left on, for garnish (optional)
4 grapes, for garnish (optional)
2 wooden skewers, snapped in half (optional)

Puree the mango in a blender. Add the tequila, Triple Sec, lime juice, and crushed ice. Blend until smooth.

Pour the sugar into a saucer. Run a small wedge of lime around the rim of each glass and dip the rim into the sugar. Carefully divide the margarita mixture among four glasses and serve.

TO MAKE SKEWERS FOR GARNISH: Thread each half-skewer with 1 mango chunk, 1 thin slice lime, and 1 grape. Rest each skewer on a glass and serve.

OPTION: Watermelon Margarita

Use 3 cups cubed watermelon in place of the mango.

# Easy Mint Juleps

On a hot day, pull out that blender, whip up a batch of mint juleps, and feel instantly cooler. My mother has a huge stand of mint in her yard, and in my family, juleps have always been a good reason to pick it. Every brunch, every backyard get-together, the julep cups come out and I'm sent to gather hand-fuls of the fragrant leaves. This is an old family recipe that has stood the test of time. To make a virgin julep, replace the bourbon and water with ginger ale or 7-Up.

I've allowed some leeway with the ice, depending on how strong you like your juleps. The hotter the day, the more ice you need.

1 cup bourbon
³/₄ cup confectioners' sugar
¹/₂ cup water

¹/₄ cup mint leaves (25–30 leaves)
4–5 cups ice cubes
4–6 mint sprigs, for garnish

Combine all the ingredients except the mint sprigs in a blender. Blend until smooth and pour into a pitcher. Fill traditional julep cups or highball glasses, garnish each glass with a mint sprig, and serve immediately.

# Farmers' Market Tomato and Sweet Onion Soup

I fill up my bags with tomatoes at the farmers' market before I even look at the other items. If you crave this soup in the winter, you can substitute 2 cups of canned tomatoes—it's good, but it won't have that sun-warmed flavor.

1/4 cup extra-virgin olive oil
2 cups diced sweet onion
3 tablespoons coarsely chopped fresh basil
1 large garlic clove, minced
5–6 large vine-ripened tomatoes, peeled, seeded, and coarsely chopped (see note)
3 cups water
3 teaspoons kosher salt

3/4 teaspoon freshly ground black pepper
2 tablespoons freshly grated Parmesan cheese or 1 piece Parmesan cheese rind (see note), plus 4 tablespoons for topping
Top-quality extra-virgin olive oil, for topping
Rustic bread, sliced and toasted, for topping

Cat's Notes   To peel the tomatoes, fill a large bowl with ice and water and set aside. Place a large pot of water on to boil. Using a paring knife, cut a small X at the bottom of each tomato, taking care not to cut into the flesh. Carefully lower 2 or 3 tomatoes at a time into the boiling water. After 15 to 20 seconds, lift them out of the water, using a slotted spoon or a long-handled strainer. Submerge them briefly in the ice water. Remove the tomatoes from the ice water. Using the tip of your paring knife, pull off the skin; it should peel off without any resistance. Cut each tomato in half crosswise and gently squeeze each half over a small bowl to expel the seeds. Discard the seeds and coarsely chop the tomato.

I always save the rind of my Parmesan cheese for soups. I drop it in, let it flavor the soup, and pull it out with tongs just before serving.

In a large pot, heat the olive oil over medium heat. Add the onion and cook until translucent, about 4 minutes. Add the basil and garlic and sauté for 2 to 3 minutes. Add the tomatoes and water. Bring to a boil, turn the heat to medium-low, and simmer for 30 minutes.

After 30 minutes, add the salt, pepper, and the 2 tablespoons cheese or the cheese rind and simmer for 10 minutes. With tongs, lift out the rind, if using. In a large blender (or in batches in a small blender), puree the soup until smooth. Check the seasonings, adding more salt and pepper if needed.

Ladle the soup into four serving bowls, give each bowl a light drizzle of olive oil, and top with a slice of toasted bread and a dusting of the remaining 4 tablespoons cheese.

# Potato–Celery Root Soup

As long as the combined weight of the potatoes and celery root is 1½ pounds, you can use a little more or less of either vegetable to make this velvety soup, depending on what you have in your kitchen.

If you spot a celery root with a head—greens sprouting from the top—buy it, trim off those greens, and use them to garnish this soup for an extra hit of celery flavor.

You can put this soup through a chinois or sieve to make it even more refined, but I usually skip this step.

¾ pound Yukon Gold potatoes, peeled

¾ pound celery root, cleaned and peeled (see note)

2 tablespoons extra-virgin olive oil

1 tablespoon unsalted butter

4 medium celery ribs from close to the heart, finely chopped

2 medium leeks, well cleaned and thinly sliced (white and light green parts only)

1 teaspoon kosher salt

1 quart chicken stock, homemade (pages 231–233) or store-bought, plus extra for thinning the soup, if needed

2 cups cold water

⅛ teaspoon freshly ground black pepper

1 cup heavy cream

¼ cup finely chopped celery root tops (optional)

Quarter the potatoes and slice the celery root into chunks about ¼ inch thick. Set aside.

Set a large pot over medium-high heat and add the olive oil and butter. When the butter is melted, add the potatoes, celery root, celery, and leeks and sprinkle with ½ teaspoon of the salt. Reduce the heat to medium and sauté until the vegetables have softened slightly, about 5 minutes. Add the chicken stock and water, turn the heat up to high, and bring just to a boil. Turn down the heat to low immediately, cover, and barely simmer until the potatoes are tender and break apart easily, about 20 minutes.

Transfer the cooked vegetables and half of the liquid to a blender or a food processor with a large bowl. (If using a small blender, transfer half the vegetables and puree in 2 batches.) Puree until the soup is completely smooth. Slowly add the remaining liquid and blend again on low speed for about 30 seconds to incorporate the liquid. Add the remaining $1/2$ teaspoon salt and the pepper and blend again. (If you'd like the soup to be very smooth, pass it through a sieve at this point.) Pour the soup back into the pot and place over medium heat. Stir in the cream, heat until just simmering, then turn the heat down to low. Taste the soup and adjust the seasoning, adding more salt and pepper if needed. Sprinkle with the celery root tops, if using.

## Cat's Note

Celery root is ideal for salads in summer or soups in winter. Milder than a celery stalk, with a cleaner, more refined flavor, celery root can be served raw or cooked, pureed, and combined with other vegetables. Don't let its craggy, brownish exterior put you off. Once you cut away the hard outer skin, the interior is crisp and creamy white.

You clean celery root much like a potato. Scrub it with a vegetable brush under running water and cut away any root stubs with a sharp paring knife. Slice off the bottom of the celery root first so that you have a steady base on which to rest it. Instead of peeling the thick skin, cut it off—carefully—with a sharp knife, then cut the celery root into thin, even slabs.

# Celery Root and Asian Pear Salad

Asian pears have a crisp texture, yet they're very juicy. Like apples, they don't change in texture after they're picked, the way ordinary pears do. Because of this, they're often called apple pears, and they're particularly good in salads, because they hold up to dressings without getting soft or soggy.

Cut into matchstick-sized pieces, Asian pear and celery root are a great pair. Both are crisp, and the Asian pear is juicy and sweet, mild and refreshing, similar to jicama.

1 squeeze fresh lemon juice

1 large celery root (about 1½ pounds),
    cleaned and peeled (see page 189)

1 Asian pear, cored but unpeeled

2 tablespoons rice wine vinegar

1 teaspoon soy sauce

1 teaspoon miso (preferably white)

½ teaspoon hot sweet mustard or Chinese
    hot mustard

1 shallot, minced

1 tablespoon sesame oil

2 tablespoons extra–virgin olive oil

1 tablespoon chopped fresh cilantro

1 scallion, chopped

1 teaspoon black or regular sesame seeds
    (see page 83)

Fill a large bowl with water and squeeze in a little lemon juice to keep the sliced celery root and Asian pear from turning brown.

Slice the celery root and Asian pear on a mandoline or cut into matchsticks with a knife. As you cut, toss the pieces into the lemon water.

In a small bowl, whisk the vinegar, soy sauce, miso, mustard, shallot, and oils together. Set aside.

Drain the celery root and pear, discarding the lemon water. Add the cilantro, scallion, and sesame seeds to the bowl with the celery root and pear. Add the vinaigrette and toss thoroughly. Serve immediately or cover and refrigerate until ready to serve. This salad will keep in the fridge for 2 days.

## OPTION: With Bosc Pears

If you don't spot good Asian pears, you can use Bosc pears in this recipe instead. Just make sure they are a little firm and not too soft.

# Vinegars

Vinegar is a brightener. Like lemon juice, it sparks up other flavors in salads and soups, even meats and desserts. Here are some of the vinegars in my pantry at home.

## Balsamic Vinegar

True balsamic vinegar is expensive because of the care and years that go into making it. If the label says *Aceto Balsamico Tradizionale,* it means the vinegar has been aged at least twelve years. I always have a very high-end balsamic that I use very judiciously—drizzling it on steak or risotto just before serving. I also buy several less expensive balsamic vinegars for salad dressings or to make a balsamic reduction (page 240). I use a fruit balsamic vinegar to glaze poultry (see Balsamic-Glazed Duck Breast, page 205). If you don't see fruit balsamic vinegar in your closest high-end grocery store, see Resources on page 245.

## Wine Vinegar

My pantry always has both red and white wine vinegars, as well as champagne vinegar and sherry vinegar. Although wine vinegar isn't as expensive as balsamic vinegar, you don't want to buy the cheapest wine vinegar out there, because low-grade wine vinegar can be so harsh it will ruin your dish (and your day). Good red wine vinegar is essential for a Greek salad made of red bell peppers, feta cheese, cucumbers, and onion. White wine vinegar is good for dressing lighter salads.

## Sherry Vinegar

A rich, full-bodied vinegar, this lends itself to hearty salads with meat and cheeses. It's a good choice when you want a refined vinegar that's midway between the big flavor of a red wine vinegar and the subtler flavor of a white wine vinegar.

## Rice Wine Vinegar

Because rice wine vinegar is less acidic, its flavor is gentle, so it won't overpower light salads and fruit.

## Apple Cider Vinegar

Apple cider vinegar has less salt and sugar than other vinegars and for centuries has been credited with aiding digestion. It's a great vinegar to have on hand for deglazing, brining meat, or dressing salads, especially coleslaw.

# Baby Greens with Prosciutto-Wrapped Apricots and Sheep's Cheese

SERVES 4

Bundles of prosciutto holding a savory mix of apricots sautéed with onion and herbs top a salad of baby greens. Serve as a first course or—on a hot summer night—as an entire dinner, with a cold, crisp Sauvignon Blanc. Kasseri, a Greek cheese made from sheep's milk, sets off the sweetness of the apricots and the rich prosciutto. If you can't find kasseri, substitute slivers of Parmesan, but it's worth asking for kasseri at the cheese counter.

You can arrange the sautéed fruit, prosciutto, and cheese on top of the greens if you like, but I prefer using four 4-inch ring molds to create an unexpected presentation, folding the apricot, onion, and herb mixture in a prosciutto wrapper. If you don't have ring molds, ramekins work fine too.

1 dozen ripe apricots

¼ cup extra-virgin olive oil

1 small onion, finely chopped

1 tablespoon chopped fresh rosemary

1 tablespoon chopped fresh basil

¼ cup balsamic vinegar

1 teaspoon kosher salt

16 very thin slices prosciutto

½ teaspoon freshly ground black pepper

½ pound mixed baby greens

¼ cup shaved kasseri or Parmesan cheese

Halve and pit the apricots and set aside.

Pour 2 tablespoons of the olive oil into a medium skillet over medium-high heat. Add the onion and sauté until lightly browned, 5 to 7 minutes. Add the apricots and reduce the heat to medium. Heat the apricots just until their skins begin to soften, for no more than 2 to 3 minutes, so the fruit keeps its shape. Add the herbs, 2 tablespoons of the vinegar, and ½ teaspoon of the salt and simmer for 2 to 3 minutes, just until the fruit takes on the flavor and fragrance of the herbs. Remove the pan from the heat and let the mixture cool.

Meanwhile, line each of the ring molds or ramekins with 4 prosciutto slices, overlapping them so the entire mold is covered. Spoon in the apricot mixture, filling each mold to the top. Carefully lift the prosciutto slices and drape them over the filling, gently patting them into place. Set the molds aside while you dress the greens.

In a small bowl, whisk together the remaining 2 tablespoons olive oil, the remaining 2 tablespoons vinegar, the remaining $1/2$ teaspoon salt, and the pepper. Place the greens in a medium bowl, spoon on a little of the vinaigrette—just enough to lightly coat each leaf—and gently toss. Divide the greens evenly among four individual salad plates. Unmold each prosciutto ring by turning it upside down over the greens. Drizzle any remaining vinaigrette around the prosciutto ring. Top the salads with the cheese.

OPTION: Baby Greens with Prosciutto-Wrapped Figs

Substitute a pint of fresh figs for the apricots. Cut each fig in half, cut off the stem, and proceed as directed.

# Salmon Fillets with Fava Bean Sauce

For me, fava beans epitomize spring and the beginning of a new season, because their flavor is so bright and fresh. Look for favas with vivid green pods and no brown spots.

This is a great dish to make with a really good friend, because the two of you can talk while you shell the favas. It takes almost 4 pounds of unshucked fava beans to yield the 2 cups you'll need, but shucking the beans is the only part of this recipe that isn't quick and easy. You can substitute fresh green peas for the favas, if you like, but get the freshest, sweetest peas you can find.

2 cups fava beans (4 pounds favas in their pods)
1 tablespoon extra-virgin olive oil
4 6-ounce salmon fillets, preferably wild salmon, skinned
Kosher salt
1 teaspoon unsalted butter

Finely grated zest of 1 lemon
1 tablespoon chopped fresh thyme
½ cup dry white wine
½ cup chicken or vegetable stock
4 tablespoons light sour cream
2 scallions, thinly sliced on the bias

Preheat the oven to 375°F.

Fill a large bowl or half fill the sink with ice and water. Bring about 1 quart water to a boil in a large saucepan. Add the favas and cook for 1 minute. Drain and toss into the ice water. Drain again and, using your fingers, open the tough, light green outer layer of the favas. Pop out the tender inner beans and set aside.

With your fingers or a paper towel, rub the olive oil on a baking sheet. Place the salmon fillets on the baking sheet and season with salt to taste. Bake for 4 to 5 minutes, or until the fillets are medium-rare (test one with a knife).

Cat's Note  I like to serve this dish with the favas still whole, but if you prefer, you can puree the sauce.

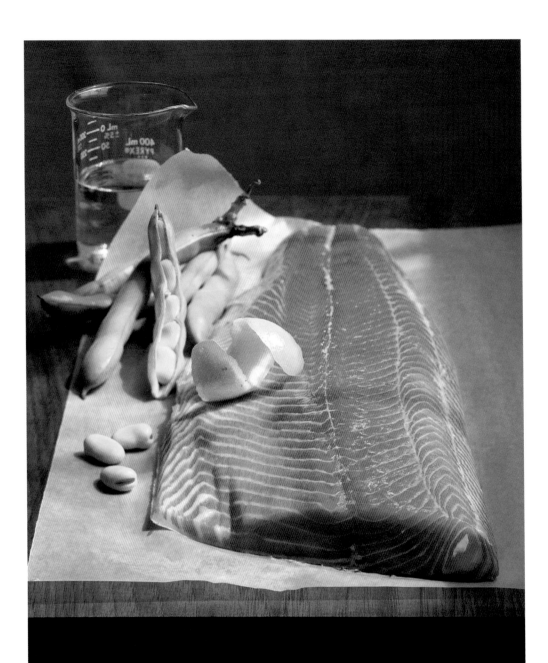

In a medium skillet, melt the butter over high heat. As soon as the butter begins to foam, add the fava beans, lemon zest, and thyme and toss quickly. Pour in the wine and simmer for 2 minutes. Add the stock and simmer for another 2 minutes.

Spoon a pool of the fava sauce onto each of four plates. Center a salmon fillet on the sauce. Spoon 1 tablespoon of the sour cream on top, sprinkle with scallions, and serve.

# Oven-Roasted Crab Buon Natale

This buttery, garlicky crab dish is easy, fast, and incredible. Dungeness crabs are generally sold cooked, and for this recipe, you'll start with cooked crabs and roast them quickly in your oven.

The dish is dear to my heart, because the tradition of crab on Christmas Eve started when I began my own family. Each year after Midnight Mass, we come back to the house for a feast of crab, white wine, salad, and lots of crusty bread to sop up the garlic-butter sauce. I invite friends to join us—my dear friend Susie Heller and her beau, Tom Stauffer, are almost part of our family—and I set aside a few really special white wines.

You'll need to put out plenty of napkins, mallets, and nut picks, as well as bowls in the center of the table for the shells. It's a good idea to set out a finger bowl and a few lemon wedges for each person so that your guests can clean their fingers of every last bit of crab.

I've included a wonderful tomalley sauce to serve with the crab. Don't skip this. Have your butcher clean and crack the cooked crabs (or do it yourself) and ask for the tomalley and juices.

You'll need a large pan that can fit 2 to 4 crabs and go from stovetop to oven. A 12- to 14-inch skillet or a large heatproof casserole does the job.

4 cooked 1- to 1½-pound Dungeness crabs
or 2 cooked 2-pound crabs (see
headnote), cleaned and cracked into 8
pieces (reserve the tomalley and crab
juices)

TOMALLEY SAUCE

Reserved tomalley
1 teaspoon crushed red pepper flakes
5 garlic cloves, minced
1 teaspoon chopped fresh thyme, plus more
if needed
1 tablespoon fresh lemon juice
Reserved crab juices
1 cup mayonnaise or aïoli (page 238)
½ teaspoon kosher salt, plus more if needed
1 teaspoon freshly cracked black pepper, plus
more if needed

8 tablespoons (1 stick) unsalted butter
4 tablespoons extra-virgin olive oil
5 garlic cloves, minced
1 tablespoon chopped fresh thyme
2 tablespoons finely grated lemon zest
Kosher salt and freshly ground black pepper
¼ cup fresh lemon juice (from 2–3 large
lemons)
3 tablespoons coarsely chopped fresh flat-leaf
parsley
Lemon slices or wedges, for garnish
4–8 slices crusty bread, toasted, rubbed with cut
garlic cloves and drizzled with extra-
virgin olive oil

Cat's Note   To clean the crabs, remove
the broad back shell first by holding the base
of the crab with one hand while placing the
thumb of the other hand under the shell at the
midpoint and lifting off the back. Remove and
discard the viscera and the feathery gills from
the body. Rinse the crab thoroughly under cool
running water, washing away all the loose
material. Grasp the crab in both hands and
break it in half; you will have 2 sections with
the legs attached. Separate the legs from the
body one at a time, leaving a portion of the
body attached to each leg for easy handling.
With a mallet or a clean hammer, crack the
shell of each claw, leg, and body section at the
edge of each joint to loosen the shell. Break off
the shell to expose the crabmeat. The meat can
then be easily removed with the tip of one of
the crab legs, a small pick, or a fork. Each crab
will break into 8 pieces: 6 legs and 2 halves.

FOR THE TOMALLEY SAUCE: Using a wooden spoon, push the tomalley through a fine-mesh sieve into a small saucepan. Add the red pepper flakes, garlic, thyme, and lemon juice. Stir in the reserved crab juices. Set the pan over medium-high heat and bring to a simmer. Give it a final quick stir and remove the pan from the heat. Pour the tomalley sauce into a small bowl and let cool. (Start roasting the crab when the tomalley sauce is cooling.) As soon as the tomalley sauce feels lukewarm to the touch, add the mayonnaise or aïoli. Add the salt and pepper. Taste and check the seasonings, adding more salt, pepper, or thyme, if you like. Set aside.

Place a rack in the middle or lower third of the oven and preheat the oven to 500°F.

In a large ovenproof skillet or casserole, heat the butter, olive oil, garlic, thyme, and lemon zest over medium-high heat until hot. Add the crab and salt and pepper to taste. Mix well.

Place the skillet in the oven and roast until the crab is hot throughout and the garlic is golden brown, 5 to 7 minutes. (Watch carefully. The crab heats very quickly and the garlic can burn easily.) Remove the skillet from the oven, drizzle with the lemon juice, and sprinkle the parsley over the top.

Stack the crab on a platter. Drizzle with the tomalley sauce, or pass the tomalley sauce at the table and allow your guests to help themselves. Garnish the platter with the lemon slices and toasted garlic bread. Serve immediately.

# Balsamic-Glazed Duck Breast with Pear, Pearl Onion, and Mushroom Hash

SERVES 4 TO 6

Fig balsamic vinegar adds refined notes of sweet and sour to duck breasts, enhancing the flavor instead of overwhelming it. Sea salt is best for the duck breasts, because it penetrates for better flavor and results in a crunchier skin.

If you have trouble locating either fig balsamic vinegar or Muscovy duck breasts, see the Resources on page 245.

1 tablespoon kosher salt

16 large pearl onions or small boiling onions

1½ pounds Yukon Gold potatoes (about 3 medium), unpeeled

2 or 3 Muscovy duck breasts

3 teaspoons sea salt

2 teaspoons freshly ground black pepper

2 tablespoons extra-virgin olive oil

1 cup fig balsamic vinegar or regular balsamic vinegar

1½ cups quartered cremini mushrooms

1 firm but ripe Bosc or Bartlett pear, peeled, cored, and cut into ¼-inch-thick slices

1 tablespoon chopped fresh sage
Whole sage leaves, for garnish (optional)

Fill a large bowl or half fill the sink with ice and water. Set a large pot of water over high heat and add the kosher salt. When the water comes to a boil, add the onions and blanch for 5 to 8 minutes (depending on the size of the onions), just until the skin starts to

## Cat's Note
Muscovy duck breasts run about a pound apiece. I find that 2 breasts serve four people; for six people, use 3 breasts. You don't need to change the amount of the other ingredients when you add another duck breast.

come off. Don't overcook the onions or they will turn to mush in the hash. Scoop them out with a slotted spoon and transfer them to the ice-water bath to cool. Reserve the hot water in the pot to cook the potatoes. Drain the onions, remove and discard any remaining skins, and cut the onions in half. Place in a small bowl and set aside.

Set the pot with the hot water over high heat. When the water comes to a boil, add the potatoes and cook until they are almost tender but still firm to the touch. Drain them and let cool. When the potatoes are cool enough to handle, peel them and slice into $^1/_4$-inch-thick disks. Set aside.

Preheat the oven to 350°F.

With a sharp paring knife, gently score the skin of the duck; this helps render the fat so that the skin becomes crisp during cooking. Season the breasts with 2 teaspoons of the sea salt and 1 teaspoon of the pepper. Pour the olive oil into a large skillet with an oven-proof handle and set over high heat. Add the duck breasts, immediately lower the heat to medium, and sear for 2 to 3 minutes on each side. Arrange each breast, skin side down, in the skillet and place in the oven.

After 10 minutes, glaze the duck with the vinegar by pouring it over the breasts and basting them with the pan juices. Roast the duck for 5 more minutes.

Remove the skillet from the oven, use tongs to transfer the duck breasts to a cutting board or platter, and let them rest. Carefully separate the fat from the pan juices, reserving about $^1/_4$ cup fat for the hash. Pour the pan juices into a small saucepan and keep warm over very low heat.

Place the skillet you used to roast the duck over medium-high heat and add a table-spoon or two of the reserved fat. When it is hot, add the mushrooms and sauté until golden brown, 5 to 7 minutes. Add a little more fat if needed, then add the pear, onions, and potatoes and sauté for about 6 minutes, or until the potatoes are tender and the vegetables have caramelized. Add the sage, the remaining 1 teaspoon sea salt, and the remaining 1 teaspoon pepper and stir to combine.

With a spatula, arrange a portion of the hash on each plate, then thinly slice the duck and fan the slices over the hash. Drizzle with the warm pan juices. Serve immediately.

# Pomegranate-Glazed Cornish Hens
# with Wild Rice and Chestnut Stuffing

SERVES 4

There's nothing like glazed Cornish hens for a special occasion, and a chestnut stuffing makes them even more special. Most grocery stores carry jars or vacuum packs of peeled and cooked chestnuts, which make this part of the recipe easy. (But if you do spot fresh chestnuts in the shell and feel ambitious enough to roast and peel them, your efforts won't be wasted.)

1 cup wild rice
Kosher salt
²/₃ cup peeled, coarsely chopped chestnuts (see headnote)
1 small onion, finely chopped
3 tablespoons finely chopped fresh flat-leaf parsley
2 teaspoons finely chopped fresh thyme
1 teaspoon finely chopped fresh savory

4 Cornish hens (1–1½ pounds each)
Olive oil
Freshly ground black pepper
1 cup pomegranate juice (found in the juice section of most produce aisles)
2–3 cups chicken stock, homemade (pages 231–233) or store-bought, or water
¼ cup all-purpose flour
Pomegranate seeds, for garnish (optional)

Rinse the rice in cool water, drain, and add the rice to a medium saucepan with a lid. Add 3 cups cold water and 1 teaspoon salt. Set over high heat and bring to a boil, stirring once. Immediately reduce the heat to low and cover the pot. Cook for 45 to 55 minutes, or until all the liquid has been absorbed.

Place a rack in the middle of the oven and preheat the oven to 325°F.

While the rice is cooking, spread the chestnuts on a baking sheet and toast them in the oven for about 10 minutes. Remove the chestnuts from the oven.

In a large bowl, mix together the rice, chestnuts, onion, and herbs. Set aside.

Turn up the oven to 375°F.

Pat the Cornish hens dry with a paper towel. Remove the livers, hearts, and gizzards and discard or reserve for another use. Lightly sprinkle the cavity of each hen with salt and loosely fill with the rice stuffing, leaving a little space to allow the rice to expand during roasting. Truss the birds, if you like. You will have some stuffing left over. Spoon it into a small casserole with a lid and set aside or refrigerate.

Phenomenal

Rub the skin of the hens with olive oil and salt and pepper to taste and place, breast side down, on a rack set in a roasting pan. Bake for 15 minutes, then baste with the pomegranate juice. Continue basting with pomegranate juice every 15 to 20 minutes, until the hens are dark golden brown, the juices run clear when the hens are pierced at the thigh with a fork, and an instant-read thermometer inserted into the thickest part of the thigh, not touching the bone, registers 175°F to 180°F, 60 to 65 minutes. During the last 25 minutes of roasting time, slide the casserole of extra stuffing into the oven to heat.

Remove the birds from the oven and transfer them to a platter. Cover them with foil and let rest for 10 to 15 minutes. Place the roasting pan with the juices on the stovetop over medium-low heat, add about $1/2$ cup of the chicken stock, and scrape up any roasted bits from the bottom of the pan. Sift the flour into the cooking juices and whisk well. Slowly whisk in $1^{1}/_2$ cups of the remaining stock. Let simmer until the mixture is thick and smooth, 5 to 6 minutes. Season with salt and pepper to taste.

To serve, place 1 hen on each plate, nap with the gravy, and garnish with the pomegranate seeds, if desired. Pass the extra stuffing at the table.

OPTION: Pomegranate Balsamic Glaze

I treat this glaze like barbecue sauce, brushing it on once during the cooking and once again when I bring the hens out of the oven. Then I put the rest in a small bowl and pass it at the table as a sauce.

Combine 1 cup pomegranate juice and 1 cup balsamic vinegar. Heat over medium-low heat for 15 to 20 minutes, or until the mixture is syrupy but not as thick as molasses. This makes about 1 cup glaze. The glaze keeps in the refrigerator for up to 1 month.

# Porchetta

You'll be sure you're making this dish wrong, and at some point the phrase "what a mess!" is going to cross your mind as you tackle your porchetta (pronounced por-*ket*-ta). Don't let that stop you! The flavor of this pork loin is fantastic and more than makes up for the less than picture-perfect preparation.

The spectacular flavor comes from wild mushrooms, garlic, rosemary, basil, and fennel, which are combined into an herb paste that is half stuffing and half coating.

You can butterfly the pork loin yourself (see note on page 212), but you can save some time by asking your butcher to butterfly it for you. You lightly pound the open, butterflied meat, give it a good coating of the herb paste, using your fingers or a wooden spoon, then roll it up.

1 small fennel bulb, coarsely chopped

1 small onion, coarsely chopped

6 shiitake mushrooms or 2 large
    chanterelles, cut in half and stemmed
    if woody

2 garlic cloves, coarsely chopped

2 tablespoons chopped fresh rosemary

1 tablespoon chopped fresh basil

1 large egg

1 3- to 4-pound boneless pork loin,
    butterflied (see headnote)

2 teaspoons kosher salt

1 teaspoon freshly ground black pepper

1/2 cup extra-virgin olive oil

1 pound Red Bliss potatoes, quartered

Set one oven rack in the lower position and one in the middle position and preheat the oven to 400°F.

To make the herb paste, put the fennel, onion, mushrooms, garlic, 1 tablespoon of the rosemary, the basil, and the egg into a food processor. Blend well.

Smear half of the herb paste over the top of the opened meat. Roll up the meat and tie it with 3 lengths of cooking twine, one at each end and one in the center. Rub the remaining herb paste all over the rolled pork and season with 1 teaspoon of the salt and 1/2 teaspoon of the pepper. (If you like, you can refrigerate the porchetta at this point and slide it into the oven the next day.)

The porchetta is even more flavorful the next day, so you can cook the entire dish the day before and reheat it at 350°F for about 20 minutes. It tastes great cold too.

To butterfly the pork loin, first find the flap on one side where the bone was removed. With a sharp knife, follow the line of that flap and continue cutting toward the center, but don't cut all the way through. Open the meat as if you're opening a book. With a mallet or a meat tenderizer, pound the pork until it's about 1¼ inches thick.

When you're ready to cook the pork, pour ¼ cup of the olive oil into a large skillet over high heat. As soon as the oil is hot, sear the pork on all sides until golden brown, 3 to 4 minutes. Much of the herb paste will come off in the pan, but don't worry about it.

Transfer the pork to a roasting pan, scraping up all those nice browned bits of herb paste from the skillet and replacing them on the pork roll as best you can. Place the roasting pan on the lower rack in the oven and roast for 60 to 70 minutes, or until an instant-read thermometer inserted in the center of the pork registers 145°F and the pork is just slightly pink inside.

While the meat roasts, pour the remaining ¼ cup olive oil into the skillet you used to sauté the pork. Toss in the potatoes, the remaining 1 tablespoon rosemary, the remaining 1 teaspoon salt, and the remaining ½ teaspoon pepper. When the potatoes have become nice and crusty all the way around, 12 to 15 minutes, transfer them to a baking sheet. After the pork has roasted for 40 minutes, place the potatoes on the middle rack in the oven. Roast for 20 to 25 minutes, or until tender.

When the meat is done, remove from the oven and let rest for 10 minutes. Remove the twine and slice. Serve everyone a good-sized portion of porchetta and a heaping spoonful of potatoes.

# Basque Beef Tenderloin

A simple blend of dried orange peel, chili powder, salt, and pepper imparts an exciting, exotic flavor to this beef. If you can't find dried orange peel in your grocery store, turn to our Resources on page 245.

The green sauce, which I use all the time with fish and meat, is a unique mix of fresh parsley, oregano, and serrano and poblano chilies. If you don't like a blazing-hot amount of chilies, start with just a quarter of the poblano and the serrano, then decide whether you want to add more after tasting. You can use different peppers with this dish too: try jalapeño or whatever fresh peppers you have on hand. The sauce's flavor will be great whether you like it super-spicy or you opt to turn down the heat.

I usually cook the larger cut of meat, because I love the leftovers, but whichever cut you choose, you don't have to tinker with the other ingredients, though you may want to reduce the cooking time if your tenderloin is smaller. The beef can be either grilled or pan-seared and roasted.

Serve with rice, pasta, potatoes, or—my favorite—Blanched Chard (page 220).

| | |
|---|---|
| 1 whole beef tenderloin (3 1/2–5 pounds) | 1 1/2 teaspoons chili powder |
| Kosher salt and freshly ground black pepper | 1 teaspoon sea salt |
| 1 tablespoon dried orange peel (available in the spice section of most large supermarkets) | 1 tablespoon olive oil for pan-searing the beef |
| | Green Sauce (recipe follows) |

Rub the tenderloin with kosher salt and pepper to taste, then rub with the orange peel, chili powder, and sea salt. Let sit for 30 minutes.

Preheat the grill or, if pan-searing, preheat the oven to 450°F.

TO GRILL THE BEEF: Place the meat on the hot grill and sear on all sides until caramelized. Close the grill and cook, turning occasionally, 20 to 25 minutes, until an instant-read thermometer registers 125°F for medium-rare.

TO PAN-SEAR THE BEEF: Pour the olive oil into a large skillet over high heat. Sear the beef on all sides, about 4 minutes per side, until it is brown and caramelized. Place the beef on a rack in a roasting pan and roast for 30 to 40 minutes, or until an instant-read thermometer registers 125°F for medium-rare. Remove from the oven and let the beef rest for 20 minutes.

Slice the beef into ¼-inch-thick slices and serve with the green sauce.

## Green Sauce

6 garlic cloves, chopped

3 dried bay leaves

1 poblano chili, coarsely chopped, with the seeds left in

1 serrano chili, coarsely chopped, with the seeds left in

1½ teaspoons sea salt

⅓ cup finely chopped fresh flat-leaf parsley

¼ cup finely chopped fresh oregano

¼ cup finely chopped fresh basil

¼ cup sherry vinegar

⅓ cup extra-virgin olive oil

Place the garlic, bay leaves, chilies, and salt in a mortar and mash with a pestle to a smooth paste. (If you don't have a mortar and pestle, put all the ingredients in a blender with just a teaspoon or so of the vinegar and puree.) Transfer to a medium bowl and add the parsley, oregano, and basil. Whisk in the vinegar and olive oil until well combined.

## OPTION: Kebabs

Soak eight to ten 8-inch wooden skewers in cool water for at least 1 hour. Preheat the grill. Cut the whole tenderloin into 2-inch cubes and follow the same steps for the rub that were given for the tenderloin. Skewer the beef and place the kebabs on the grill. Cook for 10 to 12 minutes (5 to 6 minutes per side) for medium-rare and 15 to 18 minutes (7 to 9 minutes per side) for medium-well. Serve on a bed of greens, with the green sauce drizzled over or served separately in a small bowl.

# Lamb Navarin

With baby carrots and turnips and other young vegetables in a rich, thyme- and rosemary-scented gravy, a navarin is the very best kind of lamb stew. Use only tender spring vegetables—perhaps even seek out young French beans— and you'll be pleasantly surprised at how a navarin changes your perception of what a stew can be.

Serve with hearty artisanal bread.

1/4 cup all-purpose flour

Kosher salt and freshly ground black pepper

3 1/2 pounds boneless leg of lamb, cut into 1-inch cubes

2 tablespoons vegetable oil

3 garlic cloves, finely chopped

2 medium onions, diced

1 cup dry white wine

1 15-ounce can whole tomatoes with juice

2 cups beef stock, homemade (page 237) or store-bought

1 tablespoon chopped fresh rosemary

2 teaspoons chopped fresh thyme

1 bay leaf

1/2 pound pearl onions or small boiling onions

3/4 cup baby carrots, trimmed, or 4 regular carrots, peeled and cut into 1 1/2-inch pieces

1/2 pound baby turnips, trimmed, or 2 large turnips, peeled and cut into 1 1/2-inch pieces

3/4 cup peas, fresh or frozen

1/2 pound young green beans, trimmed (2–2 1/2 cups)

1 teaspoon finely chopped fresh chervil for garnish (optional)

In a large bowl, combine the flour with salt and pepper to taste. Lightly coat the lamb cubes with the flour, shaking off any excess. Set aside.

Pour the vegetable oil into a large casserole and set over medium-high heat. When the oil is hot but not smoking, add the lamb in batches, being careful not to crowd the pan. Brown the meat well on all sides, then remove and set aside. Add the garlic and the diced onions and cook until the onions are soft, about 8 minutes.

Pour in the wine and deglaze the casserole, scraping up any bits sticking to the bottom with a wooden spoon or a spatula. Turn off the heat. Drain the tomatoes, reserving any juice in the can, and break up the tomatoes with your fingers.

Add the tomatoes and reserved juice, beef stock, rosemary, thyme, and bay leaf. Turn the heat to medium-high, bring to a simmer, then reduce the heat to low. Add the lamb, cover, and cook for about 1½ hours, or until the meat is tender. (If you like, you can place the casserole in a 250°F oven and cook for 1½ hours instead.)

While the meat is cooking, prepare the pearl onions. Fill a medium saucepan half full of water and place over high heat. When the water comes to a boil, add 1 teaspoon kosher salt and the onions. Boil until the onions are tender and the skins slip off easily, 5 to 8 minutes, depending on how big they are. Drain the onions in a colander set over a bowl or the sink. When they're cool enough to handle, slip off the skins and discard. Set the onions aside.

When the meat is tender, use a slotted spoon to transfer the meat from the casserole to a large bowl. Reduce the remaining sauce over medium-high heat, stirring occasionally, until it has the consistency of gravy, about 10 minutes. Skim off any visible fat, then strain the sauce over the meat, discarding any solid bits. (You can skip the straining step if you wish, but I like my stew's sauce to be smooth.) Return the meat and sauce to the casserole. (The navarin can be made up to 2 days ahead to this point, covered, and refrigerated.)

Add the carrots and onions to the casserole and cover. Simmer over medium heat for 5 minutes. Add the turnips, peas, and green beans. Simmer for an additional 5 minutes, or until the vegetables are tender. Add salt and pepper to taste. Remove the bay leaf. Ladle the stew into bowls, garnish with the chervil, if using, and serve.

# Glazed Baby Carrots and Fresh Dill

SERVES 6 TO 8

Glazed with champagne or apple cider, lemon, dill, and just a hint of brown sugar, these carrots have a completely different personality from the ones you pack in school lunches. This recipe works best with long, slender baby carrots. If you only have regular carrots on hand, don't make a special trip to the market: just cut them crosswise into thirds. Although the prepeeled bagged baby carrots don't have the same tenderness as farmers' market carrots, you can use them in a pinch.

2 tablespoons extra-virgin olive oil
2 tablespoons unsalted butter
2 pounds baby carrots, peeled
1/2 cup chicken stock
1 cup very dry champagne or apple cider
1 tablespoon light brown sugar

2 tablespoons fresh lemon juice, plus several paper-thin slices for garnish (cut before juicing the lemon)
1 1/2 tablespoons minced fresh dill, plus dill sprigs for garnish

In a large skillet over medium-high heat, heat the olive oil and butter. Sauté the carrots just until they begin to brown, 7 to 9 minutes. Add the stock and the champagne or cider. Cover and cook over medium heat until the carrots are almost tender but still firm, about 4 minutes.

Cat's Note    I never toss out wine. When there's a little left in the bottle, I store it in the fridge and use it when I want to deglaze a pan or add some richness to meat sauces and soups or make a marinade sing. Leftover wine is an especially good glaze for vegetables.

Remove the cover, turn the heat to high, and cook until most of the liquid has evaporated, 3 to 5 minutes. Add the sugar and toss gently to coat the carrots and help the sugar dissolve. Remove from the heat. Add the lemon juice and minced dill and toss well. Garnish with lemon slices and dill sprigs and serve.

OPTION: Vegan

Use 3 tablespoons olive oil and omit the butter. Substitute 1/4 cup fresh orange or tangerine juice for the chicken stock and increase the champagne or cider to 1 1/4 cups.

Phenomenal

# Blanched Chard

If you lived on an island in Greece, you'd hike to the top of the nearest hill and pick your own wild greens for this dish. Until you make it to Greece, you'll have to go to the market and find the best, brightest, freshest-looking chard. This is a great way to prepare it.

2 pounds Swiss chard
Kosher salt
1/4 cup extra-virgin olive oil
2 garlic cloves, thinly sliced

3–4 tablespoons fresh lemon juice (from 1–2 large lemons)
Freshly ground black pepper

Fill a large pot with water and place over high heat.

While you're waiting for the water to boil, wash and trim the chard by cutting away the heavy stems and discarding them. Coarsely chop the leaves. When the water boils, add 1 tablespoon salt and the chard. Cover the pot loosely and cook until the greens are tender, 4 to 5 minutes.

Carefully pour the greens into a colander and let them drain thoroughly for about 10 minutes.

While the chard is draining, heat a large skillet over medium-high heat and add the olive oil. When the oil is hot but not smoking, add the garlic and cook until lightly browned. Add the chard and sauté until wilted, 2 to 3 minutes. Add half of the lemon juice and 1/4 teaspoon salt and toss. Taste and add more lemon juice or salt, if you like. Add pepper to taste and serve.

# Alma's Italian Cream Cake ·

My mother's mother, Alma, was a beacon—the one person in the family to whom all of us were drawn in good times and in bad. She served this cake for anniversaries, funerals, weddings, baptisms, and especially birthdays. When I was growing up, birthdays in my family were major events; my parents were of the "this is your big day" school. My mom would cook exactly what we wanted for dinner, and Alma, already knowing the answer, would ask us what kind of cake we wanted. We never hesitated. "Grandmom, your Italian cream cake!" Off she'd go to make a moist, silky cake, with a frosting so luscious and creamy that you couldn't keep your fingers away from it no matter how hard you tried.

Two things in my memory never fail to make me happy when I think of them: my Alma and this cake.

Toasting enhances the flavor of the walnuts, so don't skip this step.

CAKE

- 2 cups cake flour
- 1 teaspoon baking soda
- ½ teaspoon salt
- 12 tablespoons (1½ sticks) unsalted butter, softened
- 2 cups sugar
- 5 large eggs, yolks and whites separated, at room temperature
- 1 cup buttermilk
- 1 teaspoon vanilla extract
- 1 cup sweetened shredded coconut
- 1 cup finely chopped walnuts, toasted (see page 24)

CREAM CHEESE FROSTING

- 1 cup chopped walnuts, toasted (see page 24)
- 1 8-ounce package cream cheese, softened
- 8 tablespoons (1 stick) unsalted butter, softened
- 1 tablespoon vanilla extract
- 4 cups (1 pound) confectioners' sugar, sifted

FOR THE CAKE: Place a rack in the middle of the oven and preheat the oven to 350°F.

Cut a circle of parchment paper to fit each of two 9-inch round cake pans. Grease the pans with butter, fit the parchment into the pans, then grease the parchment.

Sift the flour, baking soda, and salt into a medium bowl and set aside. In a large bowl with a hand mixer, cream the butter and 1½ cups of the sugar until light and fluffy. Add the egg yolks one at a time, beating well after each addition. Add one third of the dry ingredients and mix well; then add half of the buttermilk, beating on medium speed and scraping the sides of the bowl down with a rubber spatula. Repeat, alternating the remaining dry ingredients and the buttermilk. Add the vanilla, coconut, and toasted walnuts and mix well.

In a separate bowl with cleaned beaters, beat the egg whites, slowly adding the remaining ½ cup sugar, until the whites form stiff peaks but are not dry. By hand, fold one third of the egg white mixture into the cake batter until it is incorporated. Fold in the next third of the egg whites, and when that's incorporated, gently fold in the last third.

Pour the batter evenly into the prepared pans.

Bake until the top is golden brown and a wooden toothpick inserted into the middle of the cake comes out clean, 30 to 35 minutes. Set the cakes on racks and allow them to cool completely before removing them from the pans.

FOR THE CREAM CHEESE FROSTING: In a large bowl with a hand mixer, beat the cream cheese, butter, and vanilla at medium speed until creamy. Add the confectioners' sugar 1 cup at a time, beating at low speed until blended. When all the ingredients are incorporated, beat the frosting at high speed until smooth. Stir in ½ cup of the toasted walnuts.

Place 1 cake round on a serving plate, bottom side up. Ice the sides and top. Place the other cake round on top, rounded side up, and ice the top and sides. Place the frosted cake in the refrigerator to firm up the frosting. Remove the cake from the refrigerator about 30 minutes before serving, and press the remaining ½ cup toasted walnuts into the frosting on top.

# Hazelnut Chocolate Crème Brûlée

Dark chocolate mixed with finely ground hazelnuts, gianduja (john-*doo*-ya) is an Italian specialty. It makes this crème brûlée exceptionally creamy. (If you can't find gianduja, see Resources, page 245.)

For an especially crackling topping, a small propane torch is necessary. There's no need to invest in an expensive one at a culinary store; you can opt for a less expensive model at your local hardware store.

You can prepare the custard the day before, but don't add the sugar topping to the crème brûlées until you're ready to serve them.

2¼ cups heavy cream

1 vanilla bean

6 large egg yolks

5 tablespoons sugar, plus ¼ cup for the topping

8 ounces gianduja chocolate, coarsely chopped (see headnote)

Preheat the oven to 300°F. Place eight 6-ounce ramekins in a shallow baking pan or a roasting pan.

Pour the cream into a medium saucepan. Split the vanilla bean down the center and, using the side of a small paring knife, scrape the vanilla seeds into the cream. Drop in the vanilla bean. Heat over medium heat until the cream begins to simmer slightly.

In a large bowl, beat the egg yolks and the 5 tablespoons sugar with a hand mixer until the mixture is thick and light in color, 4 to 5 minutes.

When the cream has just begun to simmer, remove the vanilla bean and discard it. Take the cream off the heat and add the chocolate. Let the mixture stand for 30 seconds to melt the chocolate and then whisk until smooth. Slowly drizzle about ¼ cup of the chocolate mixture into the eggs, beating on low speed. Continue adding the chocolate mixture slowly, stopping to scrape the bottom and sides of the bowl with a rubber spatula. Pour the mixture back into the saucepan and cook over low heat for about 2 minutes, stirring constantly, until it thickens slightly.

Pour the custard into the ramekins, filling each about two-thirds full. (If making the

custard beforehand, pour it into the ramekins, cover them, and refrigerate for up to 24 hours.) Place the baking pan with the ramekins into the oven and, using a small pitcher or measuring cup with a spout, pour enough hot water into the baking dish to come halfway up the sides of the ramekins.

Bake for 25 to 30 minutes (35 to 40 minutes if the custard was refrigerated), or until the custard is almost firm and jiggles just slightly when the ramekins are moved. Leaving the baking pan in the oven and using a wide metal spatula in one hand and a hot mitt on the other hand, gently lift the ramekins out of the hot water one at a time. Cool to room temperature, about 30 minutes, then transfer to the refrigerator for at least 2 hours and up to 24 hours.

When you are ready to serve, sprinkle 1½ teaspoons sugar evenly over each custard and, using a brûlée torch, very carefully heat and melt the sugar until it caramelizes. Serve.

Cat's Note  If you don't have a torch, you can caramelize the sugar under your broiler (although you won't get the same crisp, dark disk of sugar that you do using a torch). Place the rack directly under the broiler and preheat the broiler. After you've sprinkled the custard with sugar, place the ramekins on a baking sheet and slide under the broiler. Keep a close watch and give the baking sheet a 180-degree turn after 4 to 5 minutes. Broil for another 4 minutes, or until the sugar begins to brown.

# Custard Ice Cream

Everyone needs a great recipe for vanilla ice cream. Serve this cool crowd-pleaser as is, with a hot caramel or hot fudge sauce, use it to top a berry tart warm from the oven, or add fresh fruit to the ice cream when it's almost frozen.

4 large eggs

1½ cups milk (whole or 2%)

½ cup sugar

⅛ teaspoon salt

1 vanilla bean, split

1½ cups heavy cream

Fill a large bowl with ice and water.

In a large bowl, whisk together the eggs, milk, sugar, and salt and pour into a large saucepan. With the side of a small paring knife, scrape the seeds from the vanilla bean into the saucepan, and toss in the vanilla bean as well. Cook over medium-low heat, stirring constantly, until the mixture thickens and coats the back of a wooden spoon, 15 to 20 minutes.

Strain the warm custard into a medium bowl and place the bowl in the ice-water bath. Continue to stir the custard every few minutes until the mixture is tepid. Cover and refrigerate until thoroughly chilled.

When you're ready to make the ice cream, add the cream to the custard base and stir well. Follow the manufacturer's instructions for your ice-cream maker and freeze until the ice cream is firm. Serve.

OPTION: With Fresh Fruit

When the ice cream is almost frozen, fold in sliced strawberries, peaches, or any seasonal fruit.

Helpful tips

and recipes

to make your

cooking better

Good to know

## Stocks

**Phenomenal Chicken Stock**   231

**Easy Chicken Stock**   233

**Phenomenal Vegetable Stock**   234

**Easy Vegetable Stock**   235

**Fish Stock**   236

**Phenomenal Beef Stock**   237

## Extras

**Easy Aïoli**   238

**Crème Fraîche**   239

**Balsamic Reduction**   240

**Roasted Cherry Tomatoes**   241

**Roasted Red Bell Peppers**   242

**Slow-Cooked Figs**   243

**Citrus-Flavored Salt**   244

Good to K

# Phenomenal Chicken Stock

A good stock can make a big difference in your cooking. Roasting the bones makes this one rich and flavorful. Yes, there is some time involved, but it's mostly oven and simmer time. You just place the bones in a roasting pan in a single layer and let the oven do the work for an hour. Next you brown your vegetables in the oven in the same pan in which you roasted the bones. Then you cover the bones with cold water, add the browned veggies, deglaze the roasting pan with red wine to capture every bit of flavor, and let the stock simmer while you attend to other tasks around the house.

Don't be intimidated by the idea of roasting bones and making stocks. This is not hard, and it will add so much to your cooking. I use red wine instead of white to make this full-bodied stock darker and give it more richness. If you don't have time to roast the bones and vegetables or you need stock without fuss, turn to the Easy Chicken Stock recipe on page 233.

4–5 pounds chicken bones
3 celery ribs, cut into chunks (use the leafy top portions too)
1 large onion, cut into chunks
1 large carrot, cut into chunks

3 quarts cold water (or enough to cover the bones)
10 peppercorns
1 cup dry red wine

Preheat the oven to 450°F.

Place the bones in a single layer in a heavy roasting pan. Slide the pan into the oven. Stir or turn the bones every 10 to 15 minutes. The bones are done when they're brown and caramelized, 45 to 55 minutes.

Transfer the bones to a large pot, but don't clean the roasting pan yet. Toss the celery, onion, and carrot into the roasting pan, stirring with a spatula or a wooden spoon. Slide the roasting pan back into the oven and roast the vegetables for 20 to 30 minutes, or until they're browned.

While the veggies are roasting, pour the cold water over the bones, making sure all the bones are covered. Set the pot over high heat and bring to a boil, skimming off any foam that appears. Reduce the heat to low and simmer for about 30 minutes.

Carefully transfer the browned vegetables from the roasting pan to the pot and toss in the peppercorns.

Deglaze the roasting pan by setting it on the stove over medium-high heat and pouring in the wine. Bring the wine to a simmer and scrape up all those good browned bits from the bottom and sides of the pan. Reduce the liquid in the pan by half, then add it to the pot.

Simmer for 6 hours, checking every 15 or 20 minutes and skimming off any fat or foam that rises to the top. If the stock evaporates below the highest bone, pour in a little more cold water to keep the bones covered. Carefully pour the stock through a fine-mesh sieve or strainer and discard the bones and vegetables.

Let the stock cool, then pour it into pint-sized plastic containers, cover, and store in your refrigerator for up to 5 days or in your freezer for up to 3 months.

# Easy Chicken Stock

The Phenomenal Chicken Stock (page 231) is known as "brown chicken stock," while this one is called "blond chicken stock." This lighter version allows you to skip roasting the bones and vegetables and just put everything into a big pot.

4–5 pounds chicken (whole or in pieces)
4 celery ribs, cut into chunks (use the leafy top portions too)
3 large carrots, cut into chunks
1 large onion, cut into chunks

1 tablespoon black peppercorns
4 sprigs flat-leaf parsley (optional)
3 quarts cold water (or enough to cover the chicken)

Combine all the ingredients in large pot and bring to a simmer. Don't allow the stock to come to a full boil; slow, gentle simmering coaxes out the most flavor. Skim off the foam every 15 to 30 minutes. Simmer for about 3 hours.

Carefully pour the stock through a fine-mesh sieve or strainer and discard the bones and vegetables.

Let the stock cool, then pour it into pint-sized plastic containers, cover, and store in your refrigerator for up to 5 days or in your freezer for up to 3 months.

# Phenomenal Vegetable Stock

Here's a hearty vegetarian alternative to chicken stock. If you have fresh vegetables other than those listed below, chop them up and roast them too—fennel, red bell pepper, summer tomatoes, good mushrooms, whatever. If you have fresh herbs on hand, this is a great place to use them.

For a lighter, easier vegetable stock, see the facing page.

2 tablespoons extra-virgin olive oil
5 large carrots, cut into chunks
1 medium leek, well cleaned and cut into chunks (white and light green parts only)
1 large onion, cut into chunks
5 garlic cloves, coarsely chopped

2 quarts cold water
5 celery ribs, cut into chunks (use the leafy top portions too)
2 bay leaves
1 tablespoon black peppercorns
1 cup dry white wine

Preheat the oven to 450°F.

Pour the olive oil into a roasting pan and add the carrots, leek, onion, and garlic. Stir the vegetables to give them all a light coating of oil, then roast for about 30 minutes, stirring occasionally.

Carefully transfer the browned vegetables from the roasting pan to a large saucepan and add the water, celery, bay leaves, and peppercorns.

Deglaze the roasting pan by setting it on the stove over medium-high heat and pouring in the wine. Bring the wine to a simmer and scrape up all those good browned bits from the bottom and sides of the pan. Reduce the liquid in the pan by half, then add it to the saucepan.

Simmer for 45 minutes. Carefully pour the stock through a fine-mesh sieve or strainer and discard the vegetables.

Let the stock cool, then pour it into pint-sized plastic containers, cover, and store in your refrigerator for up to 5 days or in your freezer for up to 3 months.

# Easy Vegetable Stock

Light and fresh-tasting, this simple stock heightens the flavor of vegetarian dishes.

5 large carrots, cut into chunks

5 celery ribs, cut into chunks (use the leafy top portions too)

1 medium leek, well cleaned and cut into chunks (white and light green parts only)

1 large onion, cut into chunks

2 quarts cold water

2 bay leaves

1 tablespoon black peppercorns

1 cup dry white wine (optional)

Combine all the ingredients in a large saucepan and simmer gently for 45 minutes. Carefully pour the stock through a fine-mesh sieve or strainer and discard the vegetables.

Let the stock cool, then pour it into pint-sized plastic containers, cover, and store in your refrigerator for up to 5 days or in your freezer for up to 3 months.

# Fish Stock

Fish stock is much faster to cook than either beef or chicken stock. If you have the bones left over from white fish (such as halibut, sea bass, flounder, or snapper), it'll take you about 30 minutes to make this stock. (If you don't have 2 pounds' worth of bones, halve this recipe.)

1 tablespoon unsalted butter

2 pounds bones and trimmings from white fish

2 celery ribs, cut into chunks (use the leafy top portions too)

1 large onion, cut into chunks

1 medium leek, well cleaned and cut into chunks (white and light green parts only)

2 bay leaves

2 cups cold water

1 cup dry white wine

Melt the butter in a large saucepan. Add the bones and trimmings, celery, onion, and leek. Cook over medium heat for 5 minutes, stirring. Add the bay leaves, water, and wine, turn the heat to high, and bring to a boil. Reduce the heat to low and simmer for 20 minutes, skimming off the foam occasionally.

Let the stock cool, then pour it into a pint-sized plastic container, cover, and store in your refrigerator for 1 to 2 days or in your freezer for up to 3 months.

# Phenomenal Beef Stock

The first step in making this stock is to ask your butcher for really big, beefy bones with some meat on them. Shank bones tend to be the meatiest.

4–5 pounds beef bones

3 celery ribs, cut into chunks (use the leafy top portions too)

1 large onion, cut into chunks

1 large carrot, cut into chunks

3 quarts cold water (or enough to cover the bones)

10 peppercorns

1 cup dry red wine

Preheat the oven to 450°F.

Place the bones in a single layer in a heavy roasting pan. Slide the pan into the oven. Stir or turn the bones every 10 to 15 minutes. The bones are done when they're brown and caramelized, 45 minutes to 1 hour.

Transfer the bones to a large pot but don't clean the roasting pan yet. Add the celery, onion, and carrot to the pan, stirring with a spatula or a wooden spoon. Return the pan to the oven and roast the vegetables for 20 to 30 minutes, or until they're browned.

While the vegetables are roasting, pour the cold water over the beef bones, making sure all the bones are covered. Set the pot over high heat and bring to a boil, skimming off any foam that appears. Reduce the heat to low and simmer for about 30 minutes.

Carefully transfer the browned vegetables from the roasting pan to the pot and toss in the peppercorns.

Deglaze the roasting pan by setting it on the stove over medium-high heat and pouring in the wine. Bring the wine to a simmer and scrape up all those good browned bits from the bottom and sides of the pan. Reduce the liquid in the pan by half, then add it to the pot.

Simmer for 6 hours, checking every 15 to 20 minutes and skimming off any fat or foam that rises to the top. If the stock evaporates below the highest bone, pour in a little more cold water to keep the bones covered. Carefully pour the stock through a fine-mesh sieve or strainer and discard the bones and vegetables.

Let the stock cool, then pour it into pint-sized plastic containers, cover, and store in your refrigerator for up to 5 days or in your freezer for 2 to 3 months.

# Easy Aïoli

MAKES ABOUT 2 ½ CUPS

Ultra-smooth and sultry, aïoli is a garlicky Provence-style mayonnaise. I dip French fries into a bowl of aïoli or mix capers into it and slather it on anything with grill marks.

This recipe calls for 1 small garlic clove, but you can make it with 2 cloves or 4 to 8 cloves—customize this to suit your taste. Be sure you add the oil very slowly, or the sauce will "break," or curdle.

2 large egg yolks
1 small garlic clove, minced
2 teaspoons fresh lemon juice

2¼ cups extra-virgin olive oil
Kosher salt and freshly ground black pepper (optional)

In a food processor or a blender, blend the egg yolks, garlic, and lemon juice. While the machine is running, slowly pour in the olive oil in a thin stream. As soon as the mixture has thickened, spoon it into a bowl and season with salt and pepper, if you like.

# Crème Fraîche

I use crème fraîche several times a week—in baking, as a topping for soups, or to dress up hash. Making your own crème fraîche is far less expensive than buying it. You can double this recipe if you want to make a quart.

1–2 tablespoons buttermilk
2 cups heavy cream

In a bowl or a measuring cup, stir the buttermilk into the cream. Cover and let sit overnight at room temperature.

The crème fraîche will keep in your refrigerator for 1 week. If you want to make more and you still have a little crème fraîche in the fridge, you can substitute crème fraîche for the buttermilk.

# Balsamic Reduction

This is great as a simple sauce to brush over chicken or steak while it's on the grill. Don't use an expensive balsamic vinegar for this reduction. An everyday balsamic works just fine. Fruit balsamic vinegars, such as fig balsamic, are great in a reduction, because the fruit flavor becomes more intense.

You need to reduce the liquid by half, so start with twice as much as you'd like.

Be careful not to let the vinegar sit over high heat or for too long over low heat, or it will become bitter-tasting.

2 cups balsamic vinegar

Pour the vinegar into a small saucepan set over medium-low or low heat. Over medium-low heat, watched carefully, this will reduce by half in 8 to 10 minutes; over low heat, it will reduce in about 20 minutes. Both the balsamic reduction and the pomegranate balsamic reduction will keep in the fridge for 2 weeks or more if well covered.

OPTION: Pomegranate Balsamic Reduction

1 cup balsamic vinegar
1 cup pomegranate juice

Follow the directions above.

# Roasted Cherry Tomatoes

Take a cherry tomato, cut it in half, splash it with olive oil, and pop it into the oven for less than 10 minutes, and you have something completely different from a raw cherry tomato. You can use roasted tomatoes anywhere you'd use cooked tomatoes—they add a ton of flavor to pasta sauces and soups. I roast cherry tomatoes for my Romesco Sauce (page 146), and if you double this recipe, you can also make Roasted Pepper and Tomato Sauce (page 88) for pasta.

30 cherry tomatoes, halved
2 teaspoons extra-virgin olive oil

Set a rack near the top of the oven and preheat the oven to 425°F. (If your tomatoes are tiny, set the oven to 375°F.)

Toss the tomatoes in the olive oil just to give them a very light coating, then spread them on a baking sheet. Roast for 7 to 9 minutes. They should be caramelized and browned around the edges.

Remove the baking sheet from the oven and let the tomatoes cool slightly. While they are still warm, transfer the tomatoes to a small bowl. With a spatula, scrape off any browned bits clinging to the baking sheet and add those to the bowl as well.

Stored in an airtight container, the tomatoes will keep in your fridge for 1 week and in your freezer for 1 month.

# Roasted Red Bell Peppers

MAKES ABOUT 1 CUP (3 PEPPERS) OR 2 CUPS (6 PEPPERS)

You can roast just one pepper if you like, but I always toss a few onto the baking sheet, because they're so versatile. Use them in soups, dice and toss over a green salad, pile on bruschetta, or add to a dish of cooked lentils with a little feta, a drizzle of olive oil, and a squeeze of lemon. See Pasta with Roasted Pepper and Tomato Sauce (page 88) for another way to use them.

3–6 red bell peppers

Preheat the broiler.

Halve and core the peppers and remove the pith and seeds. Set the pepper halves on a baking sheet, cut side down. Place them under the broiler for 5 to 7 minutes, or until the skin has blistered and blackened over the entire surface.

Remove from the broiler and, using a large spoon, transfer the peppers to a plastic bag. Seal the bag and let the peppers steam inside for 20 minutes. Remove the peppers and scrape off the blackened outer skin with a paring knife. If you aren't going to use the peppers right away, wrap them in plastic and refrigerate. They will keep in your fridge for 1 week.

# Slow-Cooked Figs

Fresh figs are around for such a short time that I like to slow-cook good-sized batches so I can continue to enjoy them after the season has passed. See page 181 for more about figs; you can slow-cook any variety of fresh figs. The Fig, Nut, and Mushroom Pâté on page 182 is a great use for these figs.

This same slow-cooking method works equally well with fresh halved tomatoes.

1 pound figs (preferably Black Mission or Calimyrna)
2 tablespoons fleur de sel (flaky sea salt)

Preheat the oven to 200°F.

Cut each fig in half and place on a baking sheet, cut side up. Sprinkle the figs evenly with the salt.

Place in the oven and cook for 8 to 10 hours. The figs are done when they are dark and dense but still retain a little moistness inside. Wrapped tightly in plastic, these figs will keep in your refrigerator for 1 month.

# Citrus-Flavored Salt

MAKES ³/₄ CUP

This combination of sea salt, citrus zest, and citrus juice is great as the rim on a margarita (page 117 or page 184) or rubbed inside a whole fish before you grill it. You can make this either using a mortar and pestle or in a small food processor. (But keep in mind that the salt will scour and possibly leave scratches on the inside of your food processor's bowl.)

Allow an hour or two for the salt to dry before using it.

³/₄ cup sea salt
3 tablespoons finely grated lemon zest
1¹/₂ tablespoons fresh lemon juice

Preheat the oven to 200°F.

Combine the ingredients in a mortar with a pestle, in a food processor, or in a small bowl with a wooden spoon. Spread the salt on a baking sheet and place in the oven for 20 minutes. The salt is done when the zest is no longer moist, but be sure to remove it from the oven before it browns.

Use the same proportions to make Key lime salt, grapefruit salt, orange salt, or tangerine salt.

This keeps for months in an airtight jar, but over time the salt loses its citrus flavor.

# Resources for Ingredients

## Almond Oil and Other Specialty Oils

Gourmet Country
www.gourmetcountry.com

Whole Foods stores
www.wholefoodsmarket.com

## Black Sesame Seeds

Dean and DeLuca stores
www.deandeluca.com

The Spice House
www.thespicehouse.com

## Chocolate

Brands to look for include Callebaut, El Rey, Scharffen Berger, and Valrhona. Check gourmet shops as well as the following specialty stores.

### SCHARFFEN BERGER CHOCOLATE

www.scharffenberger.com

Sur La Table stores

Trader Joe's stores

Williams-Sonoma stores

### GIANDUJA CHOCOLATE

A. G. Ferrari Foods
www.agferrari.com

Scharffen Berger Chocolate Maker
www.scharffenberger.com

## Dried Orange Peel

Most grocery stores carry it. If you can't find it, go to www.mccormick.com

or

The Spice House
www.thespicehouse.com

## Harissa

Culinary Institute of America's Spice Marketplace
1-888-424-2433

Williams-Sonoma stores

## Honey

Katz and Company
www.katzandco.com

Marshall's Farm Honey
www.marshallshoney.com

Napa Valley Products
www.napavalleyproducts.com

Oakville Grocery
www.oakvillegrocery.com

Williams-Sonoma stores and online
www.williams-sonoma.com

## Manni Olive Oils

www.manni.biz

## Muscovy Duck

Grimaud Farms
www.grimaud.com

## Point Reyes Blue Cheese

www.pointreyescheese.com

## Rose Water

Culinary Institute of America's Spice Marketplace
1-888-424-2433

The Spice House
www.thespicehouse.com

## Salt and Salt Grinders

Dean and Deluca
www.deandeluca.com

NapaStyle
www.napastyle.com

## Vinegars

Chef's Resource
www.chefsresource.com

Cuisine Perel
www.cuisineperel.com

Napa Valley Products
www.napavalleyproducts.com

Oakville Grocery
www.oakvillegrocery.com

# Index

Note: Page numbers in **bold** refer to recipe photographs.

## A

aïoli, easy, 238

almonds, toasted, and goat cheese, Medjool dates with, 7

appetizers and starters

bruschetta with three toppings, 106–9, **107**

crisped bagel chips, 3

dolmathes (grape leaves stuffed with rice and herbs), **111**, 112–13

eggplant dip, 105

fig, nut, and mushroom pâté, 182

figs with balsamic reduction and Parmesan, 177

leek and onion tartlets, 55

Medjool dates with goat cheese and toasted almonds, 7

olive panna cotta with tomato "raisins," **178**, 179

shiitake duxelles tea sandwiches, 56

shrimp and scallop coconut seviche, **59**, 60–62

smoked salmon rillettes and dilled yogurt, 4, **5**

sun-dried tomato crostini, 53

sweet potato and scallion latkes, 8, **9**

watermelon, lime, cashews, and coconut, 57

apple, Fuji, walnut, and dill salad, 119

apricots, prosciutto-wrapped, and sheep's cheese, baby greens with, 194–96

arugula, Parmesan, and prosciutto sandwich, 16

arugula strawberry salad, 10

asparagus-feta salsa verde, **36**, 38

avocado

tropical fruit and jerk chicken sushi, **134**, 135–36

tzatziki, 28

the Zoran roll, **131**, 131–32

## B

bagel chips, crisped, 3

balsamic pomegranate glaze, 209

balsamic reduction, 240

banana chocolate-chunk ice cream, 172–73

bars, date, Mildred's, 49

bean(s)

chickpea and roasted pepper soup, 63

curried lentils with butternut squash, 93

fava, sauce, salmon fillets with, 197–99

three-, salad with fresh mint, 43

two-, salad with hearts of palm and blue cheese, 44

beef

Asian steak and spinach salad, 72–73, **73**

filet of, pan-seared, with corn basil succotash, 39

grilled skirt steak with shiitake mushroom salsa, 86–87

stock, phenomenal, 237

Sunday cheesesteak sandwiches with homemade provolone sauce, 122–24, **123**

tenderloin, Basque, 213–15, **214**
berries
    blueberry ginger blender clafouti, 99
    lemon, butter, and sugar crepes, 166, **167**
    strawberry arugula salad, 10
blueberry ginger blender clafouti, 99
blue cheese
    baby greens and figs stuffed with Gor-
        gonzola cheese, **120**, 121
    and hazelnuts, strawberry arugula salad
        with, 10, **11**
    and hearts of palm, two-bean salad with,
        44
    Medjool dates with prosciutto and Gor-
        gonzola, 7
    prosciutto, and pear sushi, 137
bread(s)
    bruschetta with three toppings, 106–9, **107**
    corn, white cheddar, with scallions, 92
    crisped bagel chips, 3
    crumbs, panko, about, 19
    sun-dried tomato crostini, 53
broccoli rabe, sausage, and olives, creamy fet-
    tuccine with, 29
broccoli salad, curried, 40–42, **41**
bruschetta with three toppings, 106–9, **107**
burgers, Greek lamb and olive, with garlic
    "sauce," **18**, 18–19

## C

cabbage
    stuffed with couscous, 148–50
    Thai chicken salad with, **82**, 83–84
cakes
    chocolate budino, **170**, 171
    Italian cream, Alma's, 221–23, **222**
carrots, glazed baby, and fresh dill, **218**, 219

cashews, watermelon, lime, and coconut, 57
celery root
    and Asian pear salad, 190
    –potato soup, 188–89
    preparing and serving, 189
chard, blanched, 220
cheese. *See also* blue cheese; feta cheese;
        Parmesan
    Asiago, orzo with, 45
    Asiago, sweet red peppers with, bruschetta
        topping, 109
    cream, frosting, 221–23
    goat, and toasted almonds, Medjool dates
        with, 7
    goat, fondue, 151
    homemade provolone sauce, 124
    shaving, tip for, 109
    sheep's, and prosciutto-wrapped apricots,
        baby greens with, 194–96
    steak sandwiches, Sunday, with homemade
        provolone sauce, 122–24, **123**
    white cheddar corn bread with scallions,
        92
    wild mushroom and kasseri crepes, 158
cherry clafouti, **96**, 97–98
chestnut and wild rice stuffing, pomegranate-
        glazed Cornish hens with, 207–9, **208**
chicken
    crispy "fried," 128–29, **129**
    jerk, and tropical fruit sushi, **134**, 135–36
    and peach (or mango) stir-fry, spicy, **23**,
        23–25
    potpie with puff pastry, **140**, 140–43
    saffron honey-roasted, 35
    salad, Thai, with cabbage, **82**, 83–84
    stock, easy, 233
    stock, phenomenal, 231–32

chickpea(s)
   and roasted pepper soup, 63
   three-bean salad with fresh mint, 43
   two-bean salad with hearts of palm and
      blue cheese, 44
chocolate
   banana, -chunk ice cream, 172–73
   brownie cupcakes, 46, **47**
   budino, **170**, 171
   crepes, 168–69
   hazelnut, crème brûlée, 224–26, **225**
clafouti, blender-made, 99
clafouti, cherry, **96**, 97–98
coconut
   Alma's Italian cream cake, 221–23, **222**
   seviche, shrimp and scallop, **59**, 60–62
   toasting, 155
   watermelon, lime, cashews, and, 57
cookies, lemonade, 164, **165**
corn basil succotash, pan-seared filet of beef
     with, 39
corn bread, white cheddar, with scallions, 92
Cornish hens, pomegranate-glazed, with wild
     rice and chestnut stuffing, 207–9,
     **208**
cornmeal, 100
couscous, vegetable, en crépinettes, 148–50
crab
   cleaning, 202
   leek and onion tartlets with, 55
   oven-roasted, buon natale, 200–203, **201**
cream cheese frosting, 221–23
crème brûlée, hazelnut chocolate, 224–26,
     **225**
crème fraîche, 239
crepes
   basic, 157

lemon, butter, and sugar, 166, **167**
   wild mushroom and kasseri, 158
crépinettes, vegetable couscous en, 148–50
crostini, sun-dried tomato, 53
cucumbers
   avocado tzatziki, 28
   feta-mint tzatziki, 80
   the Zoran roll, **131**, 131–32
cupcakes, chocolate brownie, 46, **47**
curried broccoli salad, 40–42, **41**
curried lentils with butternut squash, 93
curried red snapper, 85

### D

date bars, Mildred's, 49
dates, Medjool, with goat cheese and toasted
     almonds, 7
desserts
   Alma's Italian cream cake, 221–23, **222**
   banana chocolate-chunk ice cream,
     172–73
   cherry clafouti, **96**, 97–98
   chocolate brownie cupcakes, 46, **47**
   chocolate budino, **170**, 171
   custard ice cream, 227
   hazelnut chocolate crème brûlée, 224–26,
     **225**
   lemon, butter, and sugar crepes, 166, **167**
   lemonade cookies, 164, **165**
   Mildred's date bars, 49
   rizogalo (creamy rice pudding), 95
dips and spreads
   eggplant dip, 105
   fig, nut, and mushroom pâté, 182
   goat cheese fondue, 151
   smoked salmon rillettes and dilled yogurt,
     4, **5**

dolmathes (grape leaves stuffed with rice and herbs), **111**, 112–13

dolmathes, preparing, 110

drinks

classic mojitos, **114–15**, 116

easy mint juleps, 186

mango margaritas, 184, **185**

sake margaritas, 117

watermelon margaritas, 184

white peach sangria, 118

duck breast, balsamic-glazed, with pear, pearl onion, and mushroom hash, **204**, 205–6

## E

eggplant, charred, –tomato soup with cilantro, 66–67

eggplant dip, 105

eggs. *See* omelet

endive, honeydew, and pear salad with honey dressing, 68–71, **69**

## F

fennel, orange, and olive salad, 12–13

feta cheese

-asparagus salsa verde, **36**, 38

and Kalamata olive bruschetta topping, 108

-mint tzatziki, 80

fig(s)

with balsamic reduction and Parmesan, 177

nut, and mushroom pâté, 182

ripening, 181

slow-cooked, 243

stuffed with Gorgonzola cheese, baby greens and, **120**, 121

types of, 181

fish. *See also* salmon

curried red snapper, 85

lettuce "gyros" filled with spicy halibut, 78–80, **81**

over-the-top ahi tuna salad, 21–22

stock, 236

flour, 100

fondue, goat cheese, 151

frosting, cream cheese, 221–23

frosting, seven-minute, 48

fruit. *See also specific fruits*

fresh, custard ice cream with, 227

summer combo, blender clafouti, 99

tropical, and jerk chicken sushi, **134**, 135–36

## G

garlic mashed potatoes, to-die-for, 159

garlic sauce, 18–19

gazpacho, watermelon, **64**, 64–65

ginger, peeling, 86

glaze, pomegranate balsamic, 209

Grand Marnier crepes, 166–68

grape leaves

buying, tip for, 110

stuffed with rice and herbs (dolmathes), **111**, 112–13

greens

Asian steak and spinach salad, 72–73, **73**

baby, and figs stuffed with Gorgonzola cheese, **120**, 121

baby, with prosciutto-wrapped apricots and sheep's cheese, 194–96

blanched chard, 220

lettuce "gyros" filled with spicy halibut, 78–80, **81**

greens (*cont.*)

    Parmesan, prosciutto, and arugula sandwich, 16

    strawberry arugula salad, 10

    vegetable couscous en crépinettes, 148–50

## H

halibut, spicy, lettuce "gyros" filled with, 78–80, **81**

ham. *See* prosciutto

hash

    pear, pearl onion, and mushroom, balsamic-glazed duck breast with, **204,** 205–6

    preparing, tips for, 76–77

    salmon-topped, 74, **75**

hazelnuts and blue cheese, strawberry arugula salad with, 10, **11**

hearts of palm and blue cheese, two-bean salad with, 44

herbs

    green sauce, 215

    thick-stemmed, handling, 29

honeydew, endive, and pear salad with honey dressing, 68–71, **69**

honey frosting, 48

## I

ice cream, banana chocolate-chunk, 172–73

ice cream, custard, 227

## L

lamb

    chops with asparagus-feta salsa verde, **36,** 37–38

    navarin, 216–17

and olive burgers, Greek, with garlic "sauce," **18,** 18–19

latkes, sweet potato and scallion, 8, **9**

leek and onion tartlets, 55

lemon(s)

    butter, and sugar crepes, 166, **167**

    citrus-flavored salt, 244

    lemonade cookies, 164, **165**

lentils, curried, with butternut squash, 93

lettuce "gyros" filled with spicy halibut, 78–80, **81**

## M

madeleines, corn bread, 92

main dishes (easy)

    Asian steak and spinach salad, 72–73, **73**

    curried red snapper, 85

    farfalle and herb salad with peas, 91

    grilled skirt steak with shiitake mushroom salsa, 86–87

    lettuce "gyros" filled with spicy halibut, 78–80, **81**

    pasta with roasted pepper and tomato sauce, 88–89

    salmon-topped hash, 74, **75**

    Thai chicken salad with cabbage, **82,** 83–84

main dishes (fast)

    creamy fettuccine with sausage, olives, and broccoli rabe, 29

    Greek lamb and olive burgers with garlic "sauce," **18,** 18–19

    lamb chops with asparagus-feta salsa verde, **36,** 37–38

    mussels with saffron wine broth and penne, **32,** 33

    over-the-top ahi tuna salad, 21–22

pan-seared filet of beef with corn basil succotash, 39

Parmesan, prosciutto, and arugula sandwich, 16

pork skewers with avocado tzatziki, **26**, 27–28

saffron honey–roasted chicken, 35

spicy chicken and peach (or mango) stir-fry, **23**, 23–25

main dishes (fun)

chicken potpie with puff pastry, **140**, 140–43

crispy "fried" chicken, 128–29, **129**

goat cheese fondue, 151

grilled watermelon and shrimp, 152–55

prosciutto, pear, and blue cheese sushi, 137

saffron potato omelet, 125–26, **127**

salmon and scallop skewers with romesco sauce, **144**, 145–47

Sunday cheesesteak sandwiches with homemade provolone sauce, 122–24, **123**

tropical fruit and jerk chicken sushi, **134**, 135–36

vegetable couscous en crépinettes, 148–50

wild mushroom and kasseri crepes, 158

the Zoran roll (vegetable sushi), **131**, 131–32

main dishes (phenomenal)

balsamic-glazed duck breast with pear, pearl onion, and mushroom hash, **204**, 205–6

Basque beef tenderloin, 213–15, **214**

lamb navarin, 216–17

oven-roasted crab buon natale, 200–203, **201**

pomegranate-glazed Cornish hens with wild rice and chestnut stuffing, 207–9, **208**

porchetta, 210–12, **211**

salmon fillets with fava bean sauce, 197–99

mango(es)

cutting into chunks, 61

margaritas, 184, **185**

(or peach) and chicken stir-fry, spicy, **23**, 23–25

shrimp and scallop coconut seviche, **59**, 60–62

tropical fruit and jerk chicken sushi, **134**, 135–36

margaritas

mango, 184, **185**

sake, 117

watermelon, 184

marmalade, spicy pepper, 152–53

mayonnaise

easy aïoli, 238

orange, 162

melon. *See* honeydew; watermelon

mint juleps, easy, 186

mojitos, classic, **114–15**, 116

mushroom(s)

fig, and nut pâté, 182

pear, and pearl onion hash, balsamic-glazed duck breast with, **204**, 205–6

shiitake, salsa, 86–87

shiitake, selecting, 56

shiitake duxelles tea sandwiches, 56

wild, and kasseri crepes, 158

mussels

cleaning, 15

with saffron wine broth and penne, **32**, 33

tomato and shellfish soup, **14**, 15

## N

nori. *See also* sushi
    buying and storing, 132
nut(s)
    Alma's Italian cream cake, 221–23, **222**
    fig, and mushroom pâté, 182
    Fuji apple, walnut, and dill salad, 119
    Medjool dates with goat cheese and toasted
        almonds, 7
    pomegranate-glazed Cornish hens with
        wild rice and chestnut stuffing,
        207–9, **208**
    strawberry arugula salad with blue cheese
        and hazelnuts, 10, **11**
    toasting, 7, 137
    watermelon, lime, cashews, and coconut,
        57

## O

oils, types of, 30
olive(s)
    Kalamata, and feta cheese bruschetta top-
        ping, 108
    and lamb burgers, Greek, with garlic
        "sauce," **18**, 18–19
    orange, and fennel salad, 12–13
    panna cotta with tomato "raisins," **178**,
        179
    removing pits from, 12
    sausage, and broccoli rabe, creamy fettuc-
        cine with, 29
omelet, saffron potato, 125–26, **127**
onion(s)
    and leek tartlets, 55
    pearl, creamed, and peanuts, 160, **161**
    sweet, and tomato soup, farmers' market,
        187

orange, fennel, and olive salad, 12–13
orange mayonnaise, 162

## P

pancakes. *See* crepes; latkes
Parmesan
    and balsamic reduction, figs with, 177
    prosciutto, and arugula sandwich, 16
    rinds, flavoring soups with, 187
pasta
    creamy fettuccine with sausage, olives, and
        broccoli rabe, 29
    farfalle and herb salad with peas, 91
    mussels with saffron wine broth and
        penne, **32**, 33
    orzo with Asiago cheese, 45
    with roasted pepper and tomato sauce,
        88–89
pâté, fig, nut, and mushroom, 182
peach(es)
    ginger blender clafouti, 99
    (or mango) and chicken stir-fry, spicy, **23**,
        23–25
    white, sangria, 118
peanut butter frosting, 48
pear
    Asian, and celery root salad, 190
    endive, and honeydew salad with honey
        dressing, 68–71, **69**
    pearl onion, and mushroom hash, bal-
        samic-glazed duck breast with, **204**,
        205–6
    prosciutto, and blue cheese sushi, 137
    sliced, preventing discoloration of, 70
peas, farfalle and herb salad with, 91
peppercorns, cracking, 12
pepper(s)

green sauce, 215

marmalade, spicy, 152–53

red, sweet, with Asiago cheese bruschetta topping, 109

red bell, roasted, 242

roasted, and chickpea soup, 63

roasted, and tomato sauce, pasta with, 88–89

romesco sauce, 146

pomegranate balsamic reduction, 240

pomegranate-glazed Cornish hens with wild rice and chestnut stuffing, 207–9, **208**

pork. *See also* prosciutto

creamy fettuccine with sausage, olives, and broccoli rabe, 29

loin, butterflying, 212

porchetta, 210–12, **211**

skewers with avocado tzatziki, **26**, 27–28

potato(es)

–celery root soup, 188–89

garlic mashed, to-die-for, 159

omelet, saffron, 125–26, **127**

parboiling, for hash, 76

salmon-topped hash, 74, **75**

sweet, and scallion latkes, 8, **9**

sweet, roasted, with rosemary and orange, 94

potpie, chicken, with puff pastry, **140**, 140–43

prosciutto

and Gorgonzola, Medjool dates with, 7

Parmesan, and arugula sandwich, 16

pear, and blue cheese sushi, 137

-wrapped apricots and sheep's cheese, baby greens with, 194–96

pudding, creamy rice (rizogalo), 95

R

red snapper, curried, 85

rice. *See also* sushi

and herbs, grape leaves stuffed with (dolmathes), **111**, 112–13

pudding, creamy (rizogalo), 95

types of, 138

wild, and chestnut stuffing, pomegranate-glazed Cornish hens with, 207–9, **208**

S

saffron

honey-roasted chicken, 35

potato omelet, 125–26, **127**

threads, cooking with, 34

wine broth and penne, mussels with, **32**, 33

sake margaritas, 117

salads

ahi tuna, over-the-top, 21–22

baby greens and figs stuffed with Gorgonzola cheese, **120**, 121

baby greens with prosciutto-wrapped apricots and sheep's cheese, 194–96

broccoli, curried, 40–42, **41**

celery root and Asian pear, 190

chicken, with cabbage, Thai, **82**, 83–84

endive, honeydew, and pear, with honey dressing, 68–71, **69**

farfalle and herb, with peas, 91

Fuji apple, walnut, and dill, 119

orange, fennel, and olive, 12–13

shrimp and scallop coconut seviche, **59**, 60–62

steak and spinach, Asian, 72–73, **73**

strawberry arugula, 10

three-bean, with fresh mint, 43

salads (*cont.*)

    two-bean, with hearts of palm and blue cheese, 44

salmon

    fillets with fava bean sauce, 197–99

    and scallop skewers with romesco sauce, **144**, 145–47

    smoked, rillettes and dilled yogurt, 4, **5**

    -topped hash, 74, **75**

salt, citrus-flavored, 244

salt, notes about, 100

sandwiches

    cheesesteak, Sunday, with homemade provolone sauce, 122–24, **123**

    Parmesan, prosciutto, and arugula, 16

    tea, shiitake duxelles, 56

sangria, white peach, 118

sauces

    balsamic reduction, 240

    garlic, 18–19

    green, 215

    provolone, homemade, 124

    roasted pepper and tomato, pasta with, 88–89

    romesco, 146

sausage, olives, and broccoli rabe, creamy fettuccine with, 29

scallop and salmon skewers with romesco sauce, **144**, 145–47

scallop and shrimp coconut seviche, **59**, 60–62

seaweed. *See* nori

seviche, preparing, 58

seviche, shrimp and scallop coconut, **59**, 60–62

shellfish

    cleaning, 15

crab, cleaning, 202

grilled watermelon and shrimp, 152–55

leek and onion tartlets with crab, 55

mussels, cleaning, 15

mussels with saffron wine broth and penne, **32**, 33

oven-roasted crab buon natale, 200–203, **201**

salmon and scallop skewers with romesco sauce, **144**, 145–47

shrimp and scallop coconut seviche, **59**, 60–62

and tomato soup, 14, 15

shrimp

    and scallop coconut seviche, **59**, 60–62

    tomato and shellfish soup, 14, 15

    and watermelon, grilled, 152–55

side dishes

    blanched chard, 220

    creamed pearl onions and peanuts, 160, **161**

    curried broccoli salad, 40–42, **41**

    curried lentils with butternut squash, 93

    glazed baby carrots and fresh dill, **218**, 219

    grilled vegetables with orange mayo, 162–63

    orzo with Asiago cheese, 45

    roasted sweet potatoes with rosemary and orange, 94

    three-bean salad with fresh mint, 43

    to-die-for garlic mashed potatoes, 159

    two-bean salad with hearts of palm and blue cheese, 44

    white cheddar corn bread with scallions, 92

soups

    charred eggplant-tomato, with cilantro, 66–67

    chickpea and roasted pepper, 63

    potato-celery root, 188–89

    tomato and shellfish, **14**, 15

    tomato and sweet onion, farmers' market, 187

    watermelon gazpacho, **64**, 64–65

spinach and steak salad, Asian, 72–73, **73**

squash

    butternut, curried lentils with, 93

    butternut, peeling, tip for, 93

    grilled vegetables with orange mayo, 162–63

stews

    lamb navarin, 216–17

stir-fry

    spicy chicken and peach (or mango), **23**, 23–25

stocks

    beef, phenomenal, 237

    chicken, easy, 233

    chicken, phenomenal, 231–32

    fish, 236

    vegetable, easy, 235

    vegetable, phenomenal, 234

strawberry(ies)

    arugula salad, 10

    lemon, butter, and sugar crepes, 166, **167**

sugar, 100

sushi

    prosciutto, pear, and blue cheese, 137

    rice, 133

    rolling, tips for, 130

    tropical fruit and jerk chicken, **134**, 135–36

    the Zoran roll (vegetarian), **131**, 131–32

sweet potato and scallion latkes, 8, **9**

sweet potatoes, roasted, with rosemary and orange, 94

**T**

tartlets, leek and onion, 55

tomato(es)

    and basil bruschetta topping, 108

    –charred eggplant soup with cilantro, 66–67

    cherry, roasted, 241

    lettuce "gyros" filled with spicy halibut, 78–80, **81**

    peeling, 187

    "raisins," 180, **180**

    and roasted pepper sauce, pasta with, 88–89

    romesco sauce, 146

    and shellfish soup, **14**, 15

    sun-dried, crostini, 53

    and sweet onion soup, farmers' market, 187

tuna, ahi, salad, over-the-top, 21–22

tzatziki, avocado, 28

tzatziki, feta-mint, 80

**V**

vegetable(s). *See also specific vegetables*

    grilled, with orange mayo, 162–63

    stock, easy, 235

    stock, phenomenal, 234

vinegars, types of, 192

**W**

walnut(s)

    Alma's Italian cream cake, 221–23, **222**

    Fuji apple, and dill salad, 119

watermelon
    gazpacho, **64,** 64–65
    lime, cashews, and coconut, 57
    margaritas, 184
    and shrimp, grilled, 152–55
wild rice
    and chestnut stuffing, pomegranate-glazed
        Cornish hens with, 207–9, **208**
    notes about, 138

## Y

yogurt
    avocado tzatziki, 28
    dilled, 6
    feta-mint tzatziki, 80
    garlic sauce, 18–19